LiveWell90

A Proven 90-Day Mental Wellness Program

Saundra Jain, MA, PsyD, LPC

Rakesh Jain, MD, MPH

with Betsy Burns, PhD

MW00954681

www.WILD5Wellness.com

© Copyright 2019 Saundra Jain & Rakesh Jain

All Rights Reserved.

ISBN: 9781798210833

DEDICATION

This book is dedicated to those committed to leading a life filled with wellness.

We applaud your dedication to creating and sustaining such a life.

CENTER FOR MENTAL WELLNESS
~ & PREVENTIVE PSYCHIATRY ~

This workbook is published by the Center for Mental
Wellness and Preventive Psychiatry.

In an effort to make this workbook accessible to as many people as
possible, it is priced at the lowest level permissible. All profits from the
sale of this workbook are donated to mental health charities.

TABLE OF CONTENTS

FOREWORD

We suspect you have picked up this workbook in hopes of building a healthier and happier future for yourself. You will not be disappointed. The WILD 5 program has been shown in studies to improve a wide range of measures that reflect enhanced mental and physical health. In addition, we know from talking with many people who have completed the program that the benefits transcend mood and weight: Increased energy, empowerment and more positive relationships can come from this well-researched, intuitive approach to well-being.

So, it works. But if you are like us, your ability to stick with any wellness program will be enhanced by understanding the backstory of *why* it works. And that's where we come in. As a research psychiatrist who studies the evolved intersections of mind and body, and a behavior change expert who translates academic research to the field of personal wellness, we like the WILD 5 program because it offers a step-by-step approach to harness our ancient tendencies, so we can thrive in a modern world.

What do the most livable cities in the United States have in common? What is it about these places that situate them on the future's cutting edge? The answer is surprising: These cities don't point to the future because they reflect a science fiction vision of what's to come. They point to the future because they have begun to return to more ancient ways of living. The future these places embody is not filled with robots and flying cars, but rather is characterized by walking trails, access to fresh foods, and patterns of urban design that encourage the types of close personal connection with one's neighbors that any hunter-gatherer would recognize as normative.

We have thought many times, as we walked the streets of these cities that the buildings and sidewalks were trying to tell us something important: that the best path into a human future might first need to lead us back into the past, so that we can intelligently bring along many elements of more ancient lifeways that the first blush of modernity made us foolishly believe we could do without.

What types of ancient lifeways? The answer to this question can be seen not just in the nation's most progressive cities, but also in a range of recent cultural movements that have arisen as ways to help us cope with the stresses of the modern world. From probiotics, hot yoga, and intermittent fasting to long distance running, neighborhood gathering spots and shopping locally, many of us crave re-exposure to ways of living that are more in keeping with how humans lived during most of our evolutionary history. We crave them not because we believe that life in the premodern world was some type of paradise, but because these ways of living make us feel healthier and happier, more grounded and less alienated—in a word, more human.

Science increasingly suggests that there is a reason these ways of life, ancient practice and patterns of association make us feel so much better than the sterile, mass produced, mechanized products we so often find ourselves surrounded by in the modern world: Human beings, despite our remarkable behavioral flexibility, are not blank slates.

We evolved to function best when we get certain types of input from the social and physical environment. Some of these inputs, like feeling connected to a close group of others who know and care about us, signal that we are succeeding in the task of being human. Other types of input from the physical and social environment promote mental and physical health not because they are necessarily good in themselves, but because these inputs were constantly present across our development as a species, and so we evolved to only function optimally in their presence. As they say in evolutionary theory, what was unavoidable became necessary.

Let's consider how this applies to several core components of the WILD 5 program: healthy eating and exercise. Humans evolved in a world in which they had to eat a diverse range of natural foods to survive. We now recognize most of these foodstuffs as extremely healthy. Why are they healthy? Because they were the foods we could find and digest in ancestral environments, they became over time the foods we needed for optimal health. And finding food required effort, mental and physical. Because we had to exercise to find the foods we needed to survive, exercise became good for us. This explains, by the way, why even in the modern world exercise is more health promoting when done before, rather than after, eating.

None of us has ever seen a picture of an obese hunter-gatherer, and for good reason. The effort required to find food in the wild world of nature became balanced, again through evolutionary processes, with the amount of calories these foods delivered. But in ancestral environments where high density calories were hard to find, it became adaptive for humans to consume such foods whenever and wherever they could find them, because doing this episodically promoted survival. As long as such foods were few and far between, they were nothing but a serendipitous good.

But a key aspect of human intelligence is the ability to devise methods for shortening the path to goals that are important to us. Why put in the extra effort if there is something of great importance to us that we can get in a faster and easier way? This trait has been an incredible boon to our survival and reproduction as a species, but it has a deep and dark shadow that can be seen in most of the mental and physical health problems of the modern world, which derive from the multiple short-cuts to affluence that we've built for ourselves.

We are only now beginning as a society to understand this powerful truth: Health and happiness depend as much upon the journey we take to achieve them as upon any benefit we derive from arriving at the destination. How we achieve our wants and desires, our goals and plans, is as important for our well-being as the achievements themselves.

Recognizing this is a crucial first step for attaining optimal health in the modern world, but it is only a beginning. In the days before agriculture, before all the comforts of temptations of modernity, people engaged in ancient physical and social health practices not usually because they wanted to, but because they had to in order to survive. It wasn't an easy life, but calories were controlled, and strenuous exercise was necessary to get the job done.

To be clear, humans never found it easy to exercise, to eat a limited amount of food that was healthy but had none of the excessive taste to which we've grown accustomed, to endure the quirks and shortcomings of our neighbors to maintain group harmony, or to maintain the type of meditative concentration required to stalk game across the plains of Africa. But it had to be done, so we did it.

In our time, these same practices require a level of discipline that is challenging for most of us. To make those harder choices we must, at least temporarily, renounce some of the easy shortcuts the modern world provides us – not to glorify some more perfect past, but to give our evolved brains and bodies the tools we need to thrive.

Most behavior change fails because we don't set up the necessary support structures, we try to do it on our own, and we don't fully acknowledge what we'll have to give up to accomplish our goals. The WILD 5 program tackles all of these head-on, which is good because we need to marshal every advantage we can to help ourselves overcome our evolved, and ancient, tendency to always take the easiest and shortest path to the goodies.

You've already taken an important step toward change. You didn't have to sign up for this program. And you certainly didn't have to read this workbook. Research shows that many people buy self-improvement texts, get a boost from the sense of accomplishment of having made the purchase, and then never even open the book. So, congratulations. The good news is that you're already ahead of the pack.

Normally, this good news would be followed up with some bad news: Even for those who read and make an honest effort to follow a behavior change technique, success is elusive. Private, individual commitments are less effective than public or group-based agreements—and reading a self-help book is a solitary act. This is where WILD 5 is different.

Working with the WILD 5 team, and joining the WILD 5 community, will dramatically increase your chances of successful behavior change. And this is re-wilding at its best: Ancient practices are ones that call on us to embrace community support and open, public commitments to change. You don't have to go WILD alone.

Throughout the workbook, you'll examine what you need to give up to get what you want. This is an unpopular idea, but it's hard to deny the practical realities: If you want to add an hour of exercise into your day, what hour of other stuff are you going to give up? If you want to make more meals at home, what are you going to change about your schedule to allow for the shopping and food preparation time? Each section helps you ask those questions so that you can make decisions from the start that set you up for success.

Or, following our livable city example, let's say you are relocating to one of these progressive towns. You are excited to live in a place that has more sidewalks, local shops, community events and farmer's markets – and you recognize that these are priorities for your well-being. Then the real estate agent looks at your budget and tells you that he can offer you a much nicer home about 15 minutes outside of town, in a suburb. The suburb is lovely, but there are no sidewalks. You'd have to drive in to town to attend community events and visit the farmer's market.

You've got a conflict, and as it is with all behavior change, the choice you make will determine how easy or difficult it will be to accomplish a whole host of other behavioral patterns. Choosing the smaller house in town will make you more likely to walk, build community with neighbors and shop locally. Choosing the larger house outside town will likely make these practices more difficult.

The same is true with the opportunity presented to you in this WILD 5 program. Unlike most other programs that oversell one particular pathway to success, our colleagues have made available a group of practices that, when done as a group, lead you through a whole series of some of the best understood ways of tapping into ancient sources of wellness.

WILD 5 is built from a deep understanding of the brain and body connection, and how we have evolved – physically, socially and emotionally – to thrive. By making a commitment to this program, you can set yourself up for a cascade effect of success and easier decisions in many other aspects of your life. We believe it works, and we believe you can do it.

Think of it as a journey to the most livable city around. Do your research, think about what matters most to you, and make the commitment to buy the house in the center of town. And let's go WILD... together.

Christine B. Whelan, PhD
Clinical Professor, Department of Consumer Science
Director, Relationships, Finance & Life Fulfillment Initiative
School of Human Ecology
University of Wisconsin-Madison

Charles L. Raison, MD
Mary Sue and Mike Shannon Chair for Healthy Minds, Children & Families
School of Human Ecology
Professor, Department of Psychiatry
School of Medicine and Public Health
University of Wisconsin-Madison
Director of Research on Spiritual Health
Emory Healthcare
Atlanta, GA

ACKNOWLEDGMENTS

Over the years, many people have taught us about the importance and power of wellness. We owe them all a huge debt of gratitude.

Special thanks and admiration are extended to our co-author and dear friend, Betsy Burns, PhD. Her writing genius and decades of experience as a clinical psychologist enriched this workbook in ways too numerous to mention. Her contributions elevated this workbook to new heights. We are most grateful and look forward to future projects.

A heartfelt thanks to our colleagues and friends, Charles Raison, MD and Christine Wheelan, PhD for sharing their knowledge, expertise, and wisdom regarding wellness. We've strenghthened our social connections via our many educational partnerships and hours spent talking about wellness.

A special thanks to Susan Smith, PhD, a friend and colleague, for editing the final version of the workbook and offering thoughtful feedback.

We want to recognize and thank our office manager, Jackie Smith, for her discerning eye and exceptional computer skills. She took our ideas and transformed them into extraordinary charts, documents, and tracking forms. She is not only a part of our professional family, but also part of our personal family. She reliably watches over us, always having our best interests at heart. We are forever grateful.

Finally, we extend a special thanks to each other. At times, this project required some friendly negotiating and compromises, but we did our best to remain mindful while nurturing a presence of patience and persistence. We knew this workbook would make it all worthwhile.

We hope this workbook successfully serves as a guide in your pursuit of mental wellness.

WILD 5 Wellness Disclaimer

This workbook is based on the research and ideas of the authors concerning mental wellness. Because this program is simple, integrated, prescriptive, and trackable, we believe it will help you create, nurture, and sustain practices that promote mental wellness.

The information contained in the workbook is meant to help you make well-informed decisions about your wellness. This workbook is not a substitute for personalized medical and/or mental health treatment. Nor is it a substitute for consultation with a healthcare professional.

Before starting the program outlined in this workbook, we request that you consult your healthcare professional to discuss whether this program is appropriate for you. Please do not start the program without this clearance.

Do not delay seeking medical/psychological advice, disregard medical/psychological advice, or begin or discontinue any medical/psychological advice because of information in this workbook. If you notice any adverse effects, either physical or mental, please stop the program, and immediately consult your healthcare provider(s).

Reading this workbook does not create a professional relationship between us, and the workbook is not a solicitation for healthcare related work.

MEET THE CREATORS OF WILD 5 WELLNESS

Before you begin your wellness journey, we want to introduce ourselves to you. We are Drs. Saundra and Rakesh Jain, the creators of the program. We are a married couple who live in Austin, Texas. Saundra is a psychotherapist, and Rakesh is a psychiatrist, and together we have more than 60 years of combined experience working in the mental health field. Traditionally, mental illness has been the singular focus of mental health professionals. Over the last decade, we have become convinced that this focus is much too narrow. We have expanded our view to make *mental wellness* the centerpiece of an optimum state of health. For us, mental wellness includes increased levels of happiness, enthusiasm, resilience and optimism, which we call the HERO wellness traits.

Our interest in enhancing mental wellness led us to create a program that would do just that. We thoroughly reviewed the scientific literature and discovered that there were five elements that were essential to a person's sense of wellbeing - exercise, mindfulness, sleep, social connectedness and nutrition. By incorporating these five elements, we wanted to develop a program that enabled people from all walks of life to increase their levels of happiness, enthusiasm, resilience and optimism.

Rather than creating a program that contained recommendations that we *assumed* would lead to an increased sense of wellness, we set out to design a program that we knew was effective because it was based on sound scientific findings. We scientifically studied the five elements in a variety of settings, over an extended period of time. We only used 'gold standard' measurement tools in the field of mental health to test the program's efficacy. People who completed the program had significant increases in their levels of happiness, enthusiasm, resilience and optimism. They also showed significant decreases in their levels of depression, anxiety, insomnia, emotional eating, and chronic pain.

Our research results indicate that we succeeded in creating an effective, scientifically-based wellness program. We named the program WILD 5 Wellness. WILD is an acronym, standing for **W**ellness **I**nterventions for **L**ife's **D**emands. The **5** in WILD 5 Wellness represents the five wellness elements - exercise, mindfulness, sleep, social connectedness, and nutrition.

We researched WILD 5 Wellness as both 30-day and 90-day programs. KickStart30 is the 30-day program. It is designed to kick start your wellness journey by asking you to participate in prescribed wellness activities every day for 30 days.

LiveWell90 is our 90-day program. The first 30 days of this program are the same as the KickStart30 program. While the actual wellness practices remain the same for months two and three, the frequency of practice changes. During the second month, participants engage in the wellness activities at least five days per week. The practices are completed at least three days per week during the third month.

We're excited that you've decided to increase your personal wellness by participating in the LiveWell90 program. We wish you all the best as you begin your wellness journey.

 *Saundra*

Saundra Jain, MA, PsyD, LPC

 *Rakesh*

Rakesh Jain, MD, MPH

WELLNESS DEFICIT DISORDER

Traditionally, good health has meant just the absence of disease, and healthcare has focused on diagnosing and treating illnesses. If you weren't sick, you were considered healthy. But what about wellness? The World Health Organization broadened our understanding of health by saying that health is a state of complete physical, mental and social well-being, rather than just the absence of disease. While being free of illness is good, the best state of health combines both the *absence* of illness and the *presence* of wellness.

Recently, there has been a growing focus on wellness, which is a broader concept than just health. While the absence of illness is a component of being healthy, it doesn't indicate whether you are truly in a state of wellness. Wellness isn't just the absence of disease. It's a proactive process designed to help you achieve optimum levels of wellness - *for you*. Wellness refers to living the best life you possibly can, regardless of whether you have a disease or disability.

Considerable research, conducted at multiple academic centers around the world, as well as our own research, shows there is a global hunger for mental wellness. Additionally, there is clear evidence that a "wellness deficit" of epidemic proportions actually exists. We think the absence of, or reduction in a sense of wellness should be identified and targeted. Some years ago, we coined the phrase *Wellness Deficit Disorder*, to highlight that wellness, and its absence is a 'disorder' that rightfully deserves our attention. Although currently this disorder doesn't exist in any of our established diagnostic and classification systems, it is nonetheless very real.

Is it possible that a deficit of wellness truly exists? How is this possible in the land of plenty? Aren't we living in a time of abundance? Stock markets are up, food is readily available, and most of us have a roof over our heads, and financial resources to care for ourselves and our families. Shouldn't this be enough to create happiness and contentment? The sad truth is, meeting basic needs, while incredibly important, is no guarantee for possessing optimum mental wellness.

When faced with a mental or physical challenge, this deficit is amplified. The medical and psychiatric professions, due to training, are strongly focused on the treatment of illnesses. We often forget that wellness is an essential part of good health and deserves our attention. Wellness Deficit Disorder, if present, deserves to be identified and addressed. WILD 5 Wellness was created to directly address this public health crisis.

THE POWER OF WILD 5 WELLNESS
Scientific Findings and Evidence

Traditionally, mental illness has been the singular focus of mental health professionals. Over the last decade, we have become convinced that this focus is much too narrow. We have expanded our view to make *mental wellness* the centerpiece of an optimum state of health.

Wellness is the new buzzword these days, but the concept isn't new. In fact, in 1948 the World Health Organization (WHO) defined health as *not just the mere absence of mental illness, but also the presence of mental wellness*. Sadly, this important concept was lost on the mental health field, and it is time that this shortcoming is rectified.

We began doing just that, more than a decade ago. Creating a wellness program enabling people from all walks of life to increase their levels of happiness, enthusiasm, resilience and optimism was our goal. Rather than creating a program that contained recommendations that we *assumed* would lead to an increased sense of wellness, we set out to create a program that we knew was effective because it was based on sound scientific findings. As mentioned before, we studied the 5 elements of the WILD 5 Wellness program in a variety of settings, over an extended period of time. We only used 'gold standard' measurement tools in the field of mental health to test the program's efficacy.

Because we wanted our program to be helpful to a wide variety of people, we studied the following groups of people:

- Individuals who don't have a mental health or chronic pain condition, but are simply interested in improving their mental wellness
- Individuals with a significant mental health difficulty such as depression, anxiety, and insomnia
- Individuals with a chronic pain condition (some taking an opiate-like medication for pain)
- Individuals with both a chronic pain condition and a mental health difficulty
- College students

Did we succeed in creating an effective, scientifically-based wellness program? Yes, we did. We're excited to share the results with you and hope that our findings will motivate you to commit to LiveWell90.

Granted, talk is cheap! So, let us show you the evidence. Everything we are sharing with you has already been presented at national and international mental health meetings as research presentations and posters.

Our data show that participation in WILD 5 Wellness significantly decreased participant's levels of depression, anxiety, emotional eating and insomnia. On average, people who successfully completed the program reported these significant improvements:

- Depression decreased by 43%
- Anxiety decreased by 40%
- Emotional eating decreased by 14%
- Insomnia decreased by 29%

The effects of WILD 5 Wellness on improving the HERO wellness traits are equally impressive. **HERO** stands for **H**appiness, **E**nthusiasm, **R**esilience, and **O**ptimism, all important wellness traits for great mental health. On average, people who participated in WILD 5 Wellness saw a significant improvement in their HERO wellness traits. Specifically, they saw improvements in the following areas:

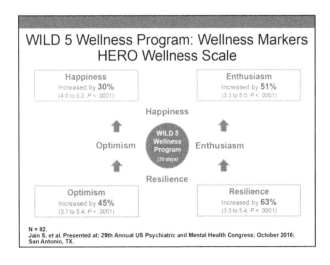

- Happiness increased by 30%
- Enthusiasm increased by 51%
- Resilience increased by 63%
- Optimism increased by 45%

If you wish to examine the scientific data in greater detail, references are listed below.

1. Jain, S., Jain, R., Kumar, L.M. (2015, November). *WILD 5 Wellness: Impact of a Five-Pronged 30-Day Wellness Program on Mood, Mindfulness, Sleep Behavior, Social Connectedness, Emotional Eating and Mental Wellness for Individuals On, and Not on Psychotropics.* Poster session presented at US Psych Congress Annual Meeting, San Diego, CA.

2. Jain, S., Jain, R., Kumar, L.M. (2015, November). *WILD 5 Wellness: Impact of a Five-Pronged (Exercise, Mindfulness, Sleep, Social Connectedness & Nutrition) 30-Day Wellness Program on Mood, Mindfulness, Sleep Behavior, Social Connectedness, Emotional Eating and Mental Wellness.* Poster session presented at US Psych Congress Annual Meeting, San Diego, CA.

3. Jain, S., Daniels, N., Gonzales, A., Grantham, S., Simpson, J.A., Veenhuizen, J., Jain, R. (2016, October). *Effectiveness of a 30-day Wellness Program in Individuals with Chronic Pain, with and without Mental Illness.* Poster session presented at US Psych Congress Annual Meeting, San Antonio, TX.

4. Jain, S., Daniels, N., Gonzales, A., Grantham, S., Simpson, J.A., Veenhuizen, J., Jain, R. (2016, October). *Description of the WILD 5 Wellness Program and Its Utility in Individuals Suffering from a Psychiatric Illness: Results from a 30-Day Intervention with an Optional 90-Day Extension.* Poster session presented at US Psych Congress Annual Meeting, San Antonio, Texas.

5. Girard, T., Klawitter, C., Bergstrom, R.A., Lopez, S., Esperanza, J.S., Nikora, R., Raison, C., Jain, R., Jain, S. (2017, September). *Application of WILD 5, A Wellness Intervention at Beloit College, Wisconsin Student Population.* Poster session presented at US Psych Congress Annual Meeting, New Orleans, LA.

6. Jain, S., Cole, S., Girard, T., Raison, C., Jain, R. (2017, September). *HERO Wellness Scale: Examining the Validity and Reliability of a New Mental Wellness Scale.* Poster session presented at US Psych Congress Annual Meeting, New Orleans, LA.

7. Jain, S., Rollin, D., Jain, R. (2018, October). *WILD 5 Wellness: Results of a 90-day, Self-Directed Wellness Program in Individuals With a DSM-5 Diagnosis and Receiving Psychotropic Medications.* Poster session presented at US Psych Congress Annual Meeting, Orlando, FL.

8. Rollin, D., Blakely, L., Tran, C., Dudley, R., Jain, S., Jain, R. (2018, October). *Wellness Interventions for Life's Demands (WILD-5 Wellness): Exercise, Mindfulness, Sleep, Social Connectedness, and Nutrition – Improving Mental and Physical Health Through Holistic Daily Behavior Change.* Poster session presented at US Psych Congress Annual Meeting, Orlando, FL.

WILD 5☆ **Wellness**®
Wellness Interventions for Life's Demands

LiveWell90
Components

- Exercise
- Mindfulness
- Sleep
- Social Connectedness
- Nutrition

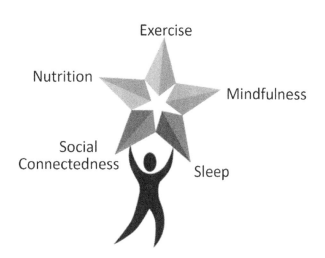

EXERCISE

Program Expectations

PHASE 1: Start	PHASE 2: Solidify	PHASE 3: Sustain
Exercise 30 minutes each day for 30 days, aim for at least moderate intensity*	Exercise 30 minutes at least 5 days per week for 30 days, aim for at least moderate intensity*	Exercise 30 minutes at least 3 days per week for 30 days, aim for at least moderate intensity*

Let's briefly explore the **FID** principles. Science tells us that brain and mental health benefits ideally occur when combining these three strategies:

1. You must exercise **F**requently. Adhere to the program's phase-specific recommendations regarding the number of days per week to exercise.

2. The **I**ntensity of exercise must be at least moderately intense, as this optimizes brain and mental health benefits. You may be wondering what qualifies as moderately intense exercise. The easiest way to know you've achieved moderately intense exercise is when speaking in full sentences is difficult. This is the surest sign that you've achieved at least a moderately intense level of exercise.

   To get the most bang for your buck when it comes to exercising, you need to know your Maximum Heart Rate (MHR), or the upper range of what your cardiovascular system can manage. To calculate your MHR, you subtract your age from 220. For example, if you're 50 years old, then you subtract 50 from 220 to reach an MHR of 170. Once you know that 170 is your maximum number of heartbeats during a minute of exercise, you need to calculate your target heart rate zone, or the optimal level your heart should be beating during exercise. For exercise of moderate intensity, your target heart rate should be about 65% of your Maximum Heart Rate. The person in our example should have a heart rate of 110 (65% of 170) beats per minute while exercising.

   There are two ways to tell what your heart rate is. The first is to use a heart monitor. The second is to calculate your heart rate yourself. You can check your heart rate by briefly stopping your exercise routine to take your pulse for 15 seconds. Multiply the number you get by 4 to reach the number of heart beats per minute. In our example, the person stops exercising and takes her pulse for 15 seconds. She gets 28 beats, which when multiplied by 4 puts her heart rate at 112 beats per minute. She is exercising with the right amount of intensity because her heart rate is 65% of her MHR. If she had been over or under her target heart rate, she could have made the necessary adjustments to her exercise intensity.

3. **D**uration of exercise requires that you exercise at least 30 minutes per day for the first 30 days of the program, 5 days per week for the second phase of the program and 3 days per week for the third phase of the program, and beyond. If you want to exercise more, please feel free to do so.

*First and foremost, consult with your healthcare provider before starting any exercise program and secondly, base the amount of time you exercise and the intensity of your exercise on your physical capabilities. During the program, we encourage you to increase the duration and intensity of your exercise, as you're able. If you're unable to reach 30 minutes of exercise per day or reach moderate intensity, that is fine. Do whatever you're capable of doing. For those with physical limitations or a chronic pain condition, you will have successfully met this requirement if you exercised to the best of your capabilities. We realize that some days, pain may prevent you from exercising – that is okay. Be kind to yourself on this journey!

TO BE FIT YOU MUST *FID*!

FID – Phase 1: Start

Frequency:	7 out of 7 days
Intensity:	Aim for at least moderate intensity
Duration:	30 minutes (at least) *

FID – Phase 2: Solidify

Frequency:	At least 5 out of 7 days
Intensity:	Aim for at least moderate intensity
Duration:	30 minutes (at least) *

FID – Phase 3: Sustain

Frequency:	At least 3 out of 7 days
Intensity:	Aim for at least moderate intensity
Duration:	30 minutes (at least) *

You may break this down into two 15-minute sections or three 10-minute sections. If you're unable to exercise the full 30 minutes at moderate intensity due to physical limitations, do the best you can.

1. Why is exercise part of LiveWell90?

There is an impressive amount of evidence showing that exercise, if done correctly, is not only good for a person's mental and physical health, but also leads to positive brain and body changes. Including exercise in this wellness program makes sense and offers all participants a chance to reap the many associated benefits.

2. What type of exercise is recommended?

Be sure to get a medical clearance from your healthcare provider before beginning the exercise portion of the program. Your healthcare provider should approve of the exercises you'll be doing, recommending any necessary modifications based on your health status and/or physical restrictions. Given your physical capabilities, any of the following types of exercise are acceptable - walking, jogging, biking, tennis, swimming, weight lifting, aerobics, and water aerobics. This certainly is not an exhaustive list, so feel free to add to it based on your interests and capabilities. Consider mixing things up a bit and do more than one type of exercise.

Participants often ask if yoga or gardening are acceptable forms of exercise. The answer is no because those activities don't meet the FID criteria for intensity. No matter which form of exercise fits you and your circumstances best, make sure you're meeting the FID criteria for intensity. You'll get the most out of your 30 minutes of exercise if you aim for activities that reach a moderate intensity level.

3. What if I'm already exercising and meeting the program's criteria for FID? Do I need to make any changes?

No, you do not need to make any changes. Just make sure you're meeting the principles of FID and keep up the good work!

4. What if I don't have time to exercise for 30 minutes?

Creating the time for exercise is necessary if mind-body health is one of your top priorities. Here's some good news - breaking down your 30 minutes of exercise into two 15-minute sections or three 10-minute sections is perfectly acceptable. You will receive the same mind-body benefits, regardless of the way you structure the timing of your exercise routine.

Barriers to Success

Below are a few potential barriers, along with suggested solutions:

Time – We suggest adding your exercise plan to your calendar and setting reminder alerts to increase the chances of meeting your goals.

Physical Limitations – We urge you to consult with your healthcare provider regarding your exercise plan before beginning the program. Physical limitations may require you to modify your exercise plan, and that's perfectly okay.

Weather – Always have a backup plan in case weather conditions interfere with your preferred exercise plans. If it's raining, or it's too cold or too hot, then exercise at home or drive to the nearest mall or go to your local gym and get moving! Don't let weather prevent you from meeting your exercise goals.

Low Motivation – Acknowledge your lack of drive/motivation as a common feeling when starting a new exercise routine. On days when you don't feel like exercising, do it anyway - no matter what! A couple of other suggestions:

1. Consider teaming up with a motivated workout buddy. Having a workout buddy has been demonstrated to help increase adherence to exercise goals.

2. Consider packing your workout clothes the night before and leaving them by the front door. Having your clothes packed and ready to go, increases the chances you will meet your exercise goals.

3. Consider enlisting the help of an accountability buddy, who you will alert each day to let them know you have completed your wellness practices.

4. Consider practicing the *5 Second Rule* on days when you're experiencing low motivation (see *Tackling Low Motivation* on page 47 for information about the *5 Second Rule*).

Words of Advice

*Perfection is **NOT** the goal! Set your goals high and do your best every day. Be kind to yourself as you begin making these changes. Change is never easy. If you miss a day or two, shake it off, regroup, and begin again. Do not throw in the towel. Remember to track your exercise practices using the Participant Tracking Form (page 55).*

"The exercise part got me sleeping better and feeling better. I felt like I was accountable to someone for working out vs. just telling myself that I was supposed to work out every day."

~JM

"I think the exercise must have released a lot of endorphins or something because it would really bring my mood up for the whole rest of the day if I did the jogging or whatever."

~ CC

MINDFULNESS

Program Expectations		
PHASE 1: Start	**PHASE 2: Solidify**	**PHASE 3: Sustain**
Practice mindfulness for at least 10 minutes <u>each day</u> for 30 days	Practice mindfulness for at least 10 minutes <u>at least 5 days</u> per week for 30 days	Practice mindfulness for at least 10 minutes <u>at least 3 days</u> per week for 30 days

What is Mindfulness?

You have probably had the experience of driving your car and arriving at your destination without remembering how you got there. Or, there may be times when you realize that your plate is empty, shortly after you sit down to eat a meal, but you have no memory of eating. When you engage in these kinds of mind*less* behaviors, it's as if you're on "autopilot." When you're on autopilot you are missing out on living your life fully and are at greater risk for feeling unhappy.

Mindfulness is the opposite of this mindless, autopilot state. Dr. Jon Kabat-Zinn is a world-renowned authority on mindfulness. He defines mindfulness as "Paying attention in a particular way: on purpose, in the present moment, and non-judgmentally."

Being mindful means you are paying attention on purpose. When you are on autopilot, your thoughts aren't being consciously directed, but instead, they are scattered. When you practice mindfulness, you are purposely directing your attention to your experience.

Being mindful means that you are focusing your attention specifically on the present moment. Your mind rarely stays focused on the present, but rather is rehashing events that have happened in the past or is anticipating events that will be happening in the future. When you are mindful, you are fully engaged in the present moment.

When you're practicing mindfulness, you pay attention to your thoughts, emotions and bodily sensations, without judgment. You simply observe your experiences, and refrain from labeling them. You approach your experiences with non-judgment, allowing them to be as they are, rather than evaluating whether they are good or bad.

Whether you're new to mindfulness, have dabbled in it a bit, or are a seasoned meditator, the benefits of a mindfulness-based practice are supported scientifically by thousands of research studies documenting its benefits. Data tell us that a regular mindfulness practice improves both mental and physical health. If you're new to a mindfulness-based practice, please don't feel overwhelmed or have thoughts such as – "I will never learn how to do it "right." I can tell that this is going to be too difficult for me." As LiveWell90 will demonstrate, learning mindfulness is not an intimidating process, and you simply can't do it "wrong." Even with 30 days of regular mindfulness practice, you can expect a positive impact. The data on mindfulness helping us deal with mood and anxiety, increasing our overall sense of well-being, and improving our health are solid and convincing. Please don't shy away if mindfulness strikes you as a 'New Age, mystical' practice. Remember, it's a top-notch wellness intervention, supported by many research studies documenting its benefits!

Mindfulness Meditations

During your LiveWell90 journey, you will be asked to listen to guided mindfulness meditations. The mindfulness meditation options you can choose from include:

- WILD 5 Wellness Meditations (more details below)
- Online meditation apps
- If you're already meditating, please continue your practice.

WILD 5 Wellness Meditations

Prior to beginning the program, please listen to meditations 1 through 6 to become familiar with each. You may use any combination of these meditations to fulfill the program expectations. The meditations are available online at:

> **www.wild5meditations.com**

You may download these to your smartphone, computer, tablet, or play them on your computer.

1. Five-Minute Breathing Space (6:45)
2. Mindful Breathing (15:00)
3. Body Scan (15:00)
4. A Moment of Gratitude (9:58)
5. Happiness Meditation (11:37)
6. Pain Meditation (13:00)

Online Meditation Apps

There are many meditation apps available online, so please feel free to investigate the various options. To help in your search, the app below is one we recommend:

STOP BREATHE & THINK

Scientific evidence has shown that you can develop kindness and compassion by focusing on these attitudes through the practice of mindfulness meditation.

Highlights:

- Mindfulness, meditation, and compassion building tool
- Assesses your current state and then provides a list of relevant meditations
- A variety of free meditations available
- Self-meditation timer
- iOS, Android, and web versions available

Practice Recommendations

1. Find a place to meditate: Select a quiet and comfortable place to meditate. To ensure that you're not interrupted, notify your family and friends that you'll be unavailable during your meditation time. A ringing phone is disruptive, so consider leaving your phone in another room or on silent.

2. Select your sitting equipment: There are three options – chair, firm cushion on the floor, or a meditation bench. Please investigate each of these options and select your favorite.

3. Decide when you will meditate. You may want to meditate at the same time each day. Time is the most common barrier, so setting aside a specific time may be helpful.

4. We encourage you to find a time that works best with your schedule. Add this to your calendar with alert reminders.

Adapted from: Teasdale J., Williams M. and Segal Z. (2014) *The Mindful Workbook.* New York, New York: Guilford Publications, Inc.

FAQs

1. Why is mindfulness part of LiveWell90?

There is extremely solid evidence supporting the effectiveness of mindfulness in improving overall mental and physical wellness. There is now convincing evidence that those that regularly practice mindfulness can change the size and functioning of their brains. Mindfulness also alters and improves immune functioning. Best of all, regular mindfulness practice makes us more resilient and improves our wellbeing. It's a star member of LiveWell90!

2. I have never practiced mindfulness. I'm too intimidated to begin. How do I get started?

You're not alone - we completely understand! Please know that despite these hesitations, anyone can begin and grow a mindfulness-based practice. You have several options regarding which guided meditations to use:

- WILD 5 Wellness Meditations (for those new to the practice)
- Online meditation apps

- If you're already meditating, please continue your practice
- And most importantly, please remember these few things:
    - There is simply no such thing as a good or bad mindfulness practice session.
    - Distractions during mindfulness practice are expected! Please don't criticize yourself if your mind wanders. Even the Dalai Lama talks about his mind wandering during meditation.
    - The benefits of mindfulness meditation are cumulative, continuing to increase, the more you practice.

3. Is there a right or wrong way to practice mindfulness?

You'll be glad to know that it is not possible to practice mindfulness a right or wrong way. Your mind may frequently wander during some practices, and less during others. This doesn't make one practice better than another – they simply are what they are. Keep in mind that one element of mindfulness is being non-judgmental. The mind wandering is in fact what the mind does quite naturally. It is not a sign of doing the practice incorrectly. As you begin your mindfulness practice, be kind to yourself and make it a priority to practice consistently.

4. Why is consistent practice important?

There are a couple of reasons why consistent practice is important. First, developing a new habit requires consistency. Secondly, it's regular practice that creates lasting positive changes both in your body and brain, and in your mental health. So, having a regular practice is vitally important - please commit to practicing consistently!

Barriers to Success

Below are a few potential barriers along with suggested solutions:

Time – We suggest adding your mindfulness-based meditation practice plan to your calendar and set reminder alerts to ensure that you meet your goals. To avoid interruptions, let family and friends know when you will be meditating.

Low Motivation – Acknowledge your lack of drive/motivation as a common feeling when beginning your mindfulness-based practice. On days when you don't feel like meditating, or you are struggling with the practice, make it happen anyway - no matter what! Remember, when you are doing your mindfulness-based meditation, you may encounter feelings of frustration or boredom. No matter what feelings you encounter - good, bad, or indifferent - stick with the practice, knowing there is no right or wrong way to meditate. A couple of other suggestions:

1. Consider enlisting the help of an accountability buddy; someone you'll alert each day letting them know you've completed your wellness practices, and

2. Consider practicing the *5 Second Rule* on days when you're experiencing low motivation (see *Tackling Low Motivation* on page 47 for information about the *5 Second Rule*).

Words of Advice

*Perfection is **NOT** the goal! Set your goals high and do your best every day. Be kind to yourself as you begin making these changes. Change is never easy. If you miss a day or two, shake it off, regroup, and begin again. Do not throw in the towel. Remember to track your mindfulness practices using the Participant Tracking Form (page 55).*

What Others are Saying

"I have not done mindful meditation in the past and this program has really helped me to do this. We have sometimes done the meditation early (before I have really woken up) and I am semi-awake for the time. I am doing more breathing meditations and really like both the Gratitude and the Happiness meditations. We are still using them, even after the program."

~ LS

"I attempt to take time everyday to meditate, do deep breathing and stretching. It really starts my day off well."

~ LB

SLEEP

Program Expectations		
PHASE 1: Start	**PHASE 2: Solidify**	**PHASE 3: Sustain**
Implement 4 or more of the 6 sleep hygiene practices <u>each day</u> for 30 days	Implement 4 or more of the 6 sleep hygiene practices <u>at least 5 days</u> per week for 30 days	Implement 4 or more of the 6 sleep hygiene practices <u>at least 3 days</u> per week for 30 days

Data tell us that sleep is crucial for overall good health. Lack of sleep or poor-quality sleep is connected to increased inflammation, which is associated with a host of health problems including poor daytime concentration and productivity, weight gain, and pain, to name just a few. Insomnia increases the risk for *nearly every* mental health and physical health issue. Therefore, we MUST all learn to sleep better. This is not optional - nature makes it a *mandate*.

The list below describes the 6 sleep hygiene practices, all of which are known to improve a person's overall quality of sleep. While implementing all 6 sleep hygiene practices each day/night is ideal, it is not required. However, you must implement 4 or more of the 6 sleep hygiene practices to successfully meet the program requirements for this element. We encourage you to practice as many of these as you can. Please don't avoid those you think you can't master. Give them a try - you may be pleasantly surprised.

6 Sleep Hygiene Practices

1. Due to the light they emit, avoid all electronic devices (e.g., television, smartphones, online games, tablets, computers, e-readers) 90 minutes prior to bedtime. If you read before going to bed, stick to content that is upbeat and positive. Reading disturbing material may cause overstimulation.

2. Avoid napping during the day. No matter how tired you are during the day, resist the temptation of a quick nap as this only results in poor nighttime sleep.

3. Eliminate ambient light in your bedroom (e.g., light from a clock radio, cell phone, windows). Try blackout shades and/or a night mask to block out all light.

4. Enjoy a warm relaxing bath or shower prior to bedtime.

5. Establish and stick to a regular bedtime each night, including weekends.

6. Avoid caffeinated drinks 10 hours before bedtime.

1. I'm confused about logging my sleep practices on the *Participant Tracking Form*? What if I only implemented 2 of the 6 sleep hygiene practices?

LiveWell90 has 6 sleep hygiene practices. To successfully meet the program requirements, you must implement 4 or more of these 6 practices. So, if you only implemented 2 of the 6 sleep hygiene practices, then you did not meet the program requirement.

2. There's no way I can avoid caffeinated drinks 10 hours before bedtime. What should I do?

We understand this is one of the more challenging sleep hygiene recommendations. It's important not to avoid recommendations that present the biggest barrier. Accept the fact that avoiding caffeinated drinks 10 hours before bedtime won't be easy but give it a try anyway. If your caffeine consumption is extremely high, you may have to start slowly at first to avoid withdrawal symptoms, like headaches. Remember, you have some wiggle room. You are only being asked to implement 4 or more of the 6 sleep hygiene practices to successfully meet the program requirements for this element.

3. Is lack of sleep associated with weight gain?

Absolutely! Not only is lack of sleep associated with weight gain but also attempts to lose weight are less effective for those who don't sleep well. Now you can see the value of a wellness intervention that combines several elements. If you're working hard to lose weight but not sleeping well, you simply won't get the results you desire.

4. Why is napping a bad idea?

Breaking the habit of napping can be challenging. However, if you continue to nap, you're guaranteed disrupted and fragmented sleep. To ensure quality sleep, you must stop napping. As you begin breaking this habit, you may feel extreme exhaustion. If you do, push through it, resist the urge to nap, and ultimately you will experience the joys of restful sleep. This is a process, so please don't expect immediate changes in the quality of your sleep. You will establish a very powerful pro-sleep practice if you eliminate napping during your 90-day program.

5. Why do I have to avoid using all electronic devices 90 minutes before bedtime?

Melatonin is the body's natural sleep hormone and helps to regulate your sleep and waking cycles. A small gland in the brain called the pineal gland begins releasing melatonin about 90 minutes before your regular bedtime. Any light - but especially the blue light which is emitted from electronic devices such as smartphones, televisions, computers and tablets - can prevent the pineal gland from releasing melatonin. When this happens, your sleep will be negatively impacted.

6. Why is ambient light a problem?

As was explained in answer 5, your body's ability to produce melatonin is an essential component of quality sleep. Your exposure to any ambient light - a night light, a clock radio, a hallway light, light emitted from an electronic device - suppresses melatonin production, and that will adversely affect your sleep. Ideally, there should be no ambient light in your bedroom. It can be eliminated completely by using blackout shades and/or a sleep mask. Don't underestimate the disrupting effect ambient light has on your sleep.

Barriers to Success

Below are a few potential barriers along with suggested solutions:

Time – Once you implement some of the sleep hygiene practices, there's little left to do except close the shades and/or put on a sleep mask. Once you decide on your bedtime, we suggest adding it to your calendar with two reminder alerts:

1. 90 minutes prior to your bedtime an alert to shut off all electronics in preparation for bedtime, and

2. 15 minutes prior to bedtime an alert to begin bedtime preparations.

Other sleep hygiene practices require behavioral changes, but no extra time (e.g., no daytime napping, no caffeinated drinks 10 hours before bedtime).

Low Motivation – Acknowledge your lack of drive/motivation as a common feeling when deciding to change your sleep habits. On days when you want to take a quick nap, have a cup of coffee late in the afternoon, or check your phone for messages at bedtime, stick to your sleep hygiene practices - no matter what! A couple of other suggestions:

1. Consider enlisting the help of an accountability buddy; someone you'll alert each day letting them know you've completed your wellness practices, and

2. Consider practicing the *5 Second Rule* on days when you're experiencing low motivation (see *Tackling Low Motivation* on page 47 for information about the *5 Second Rule*).

Words of Advice

*Perfection is **NOT** the goal! Set your goals high and do your best every day. Be kind to yourself as you begin making these changes. Change is never easy. If you miss a day or two, shake it off, regroup, and begin again. Do not throw in the towel. Remember to track your sleep practices using the Participant Tracking Form (page 55).*

What Others are Saying

"Incorporation of the 5 wellness practices has enhanced my life! I never thought I could get away from napping on the weekends, but it has become a reality! I also have more mental clarity and energy as a result of the 5 wellness practices combined."

~AC

"This was a wonderful and enlightening experience as I balanced all five elements of wellness practices that were already a part of my life. Our culture is at new heights of stress and sleep problems. Little did I know how internet modem lights flashing my direction all night while I tried to sleep could play such a role in my poor sleep quality. What a revelation that the world needs to hear!!"

~CZ

SOCIAL CONNECTEDNESS

Program Expectations		
PHASE 1: Start	**PHASE 2: Solidify**	**PHASE 3: Sustain**
Meet or call a minimum of two friends or family members <u>each day</u> for 30 days	Meet or call a minimum of two friends or family members <u>at least 5 days</u> per week for 30 days	Meet or call a minimum of two friends or family members <u>at least 3 days</u> per week for 30 days

Humans are social animals, but the hectic pace of modern life often gets in the way of our efforts to connect with others. This is important because socialization is essential to both mental and physical health. Data tell us that people who socialize more frequently live longer, have fewer health problems, and are happier. Given the power of socialization, it is one of the five wellness elements.

The science behind socialization as a wellness technique is massive. Social isolation is at an epidemic level in our society, and this comes with a very heavy price tag – higher rates of depression and anxiety, increased risk of cardiovascular problems, and a higher risk of obesity. In other words, being even somewhat socially disconnected harms your mind, brain, and body. The good news is that individuals who consciously increase both the quality and quantity of their social interactions see benefits in all the areas outlined above. Socialization, without a doubt, positively impacts your mind-body health and wellbeing.

We'd like to introduce you to a new way of thinking about socialization. It involves two concepts that you may not be familiar with - *macro-* and *micro*-socialization.

By *macro*-socialization we mean engaging in social activities with friends and family members over a period of months, years and even a lifetime. Here are some examples of macro-socialization activities:

- Having dinner with family or friends
- Seeing a movie with family or friends
- Having coffee with family or friends
- Taking a walk with family or friends
- Joining a book club
- Participating in a sporting activity, such as tennis, basketball, racquetball
- Taking a cooking class or a dance class with family or friends

Micro-socialization refers to brief, social interactions with strangers or casual acquaintances. Examples include saying good morning as you pass someone, smiling as someone approaches, and greeting people at the grocery store or on an elevator.

Today people are engaging in fewer macro- and micro-socialization activities. We urge you to become more mindful of your own macro- and micro-socialization habits and examine any barriers you may have to optimizing both.

To meet the social connectedness component of the program, you will be asked to meet or call a minimum of two friends or family members. You don't have to record any details about your socialization experiences except to document your practices using your *Participant Tracking Form* (page 55).

You may be wondering why texting isn't an option for socially connecting with others. Here's our reasoning. In one of our recently completed studies at a college in Wisconsin, we found the number of students who successfully met the requirements for the social connectedness element was quite high. However, the students' pre-post scores on their sense of connectedness showed no improvement. So, college-age participants, those we suspected would be very connected socially, showed no improvement in their sense of connectedness when texting was an approved method for socializing. A faculty member involved with the study, pointed out that texting is not a true form of connection. Students met the program requirements for social connectedness but lost out in terms of feeling more connected to others, their communities, and their families. Based on these findings, we felt it was important to remove texting as an option to meet the social connectedness program requirements.

FAQs

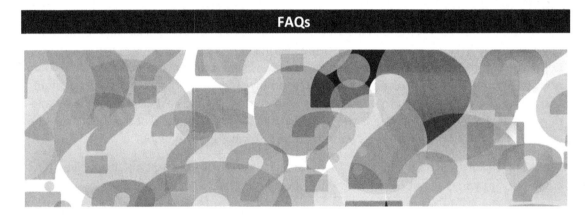

1. I don't like talking on the phone. It makes me uncomfortable. What should I do?

We realize not everyone likes talking on the phone. If speaking on the phone makes you uncomfortable, do your best to do it anyway. The more you engage in this activity, the easier it will become. Don't always do what's easiest – push yourself to break out of your comfort zone. We recommend you do both - call others and meet face-to-face; try mixing it up a bit.

2. This seems too easy. How can it be helpful?

Take a moment and consider what previous participants have said about this wellness element. Their feedback opened our eyes to the power of this intervention...see what you think. Before starting the program, one participant felt she was very connected. However, once she started tracking her socialization practices, she realized she wasn't connecting with others as often as she thought. So, tracking increased her awareness and offered her an opportunity to change her behavior. Another participant was extremely isolated and something as simple as calling others, allowed him to engage in behavior that increased his level of social connectedness. So, please don't underestimate this intervention because of its simplicity.

3. "Macro-socialization" and "micro-socialization" are new concepts to me. Would you explain what they mean and how they apply to LiveWell90?

Macro-socialization (large): Engaging in big social activities like joining a group or spending significant amounts of time with friends and family, over a period of months, years, or even a lifetime.

Micro-socialization (small): Interacting with strangers or casual acquaintances in brief social interactions - nodding pleasantly, smiling as someone approaches, or saying good morning. As an example, while on an elevator, do you interact with others or avoid eye-contact while quietly waiting for your floor? If you avoid others on the elevator, you've just missed out on an opportunity to engage in a micro-socialization activity.

Both macro- and micro-socialization are powerful ways to boost your mental wellness. We encourage you to grab every opportunity to engage in both. Practice stepping outside of your comfort zone and give both styles of interaction a try. The benefits to your mental wellness will be worth the effort.

4. I don't have the time to meet face-to-face with friends or family. I'm just too busy. What should I do?

We realize hectic schedules make it difficult to find time to connect face-to-face. If you're not yet convinced of the power of socialization, we encourage you to review this element. If you want to improve your overall mental and physical wellbeing, you must overcome this barrier and make time to connect. The benefits far outweigh the hassle factor. There is power in meeting face-to-face, and spending quality time together in person. When that's not possible, connecting via phone is a viable option.

5. Do I need to keep track of the people I meet or call, as well as the content of the communications?

No, you don't need to keep records. Simply log your practices using your *Participant Tracking Form* (page 55).

Barriers to Success

Below are a few potential barriers along with suggested solutions:

Time – We suggest adding your social connectedness activities to your calendar and set reminder alerts to increase the chances of meeting your goals.

Low Motivation – Acknowledge your lack of drive/motivation as a common feeling when deciding to socialize. On days when you feel avoidant or less than social, do your socialization activities anyway - no matter what! A couple of other suggestions:

1. Consider enlisting the help of an accountability buddy; someone you'll alert each day letting them know you've completed your wellness practices, and

2. Consider practicing the *5 Second Rule* on days when you're experiencing low motivation (see *Tackling Low Motivation* on page 47 for information about the *5 Second Rule*).

Words of Advice

*Perfection is **NOT** the goal! Set your goals high and do your best every day. Be kind to yourself as you begin making these changes. Change is never easy. If you miss a day or two, shake it off, regroup, and begin again. Do not throw in the towel. Remember to track your social connectedness practices using the Participant Tracking Form (page 55).*

What Others are Saying

"I enjoyed the social connection piece, as I went into the program feeling somewhat "isolated" after I retired - spent most of my time at home (or though it seemed). I was pleased to find out that my social connections were present every day. I was also reaching out to more friends by text and by written notes than I had been able to do in the past while working. The connections were positive and very satisfying."

~LS

"A great transformation for me in terms of social contact. Needing to follow through helped me get over my reticence to call people in the evenings. My life is much richer."

~ RR

NUTRITION

Program Expectations

PHASE 1: Start	PHASE 2: Solidify	PHASE 3: Sustain
Log your meals/ snacks/beverages/alcohol <u>each day</u> for 30 days [Follow the MIND diet principles as closely as you can]	Log your meals/ snacks/beverages/alcohol <u>at least 5 days</u> per week for 30 days [Follow the MIND diet principles as closely as you can]	Log your meals/ snacks/beverages/alcohol <u>at least 3 days</u> per week for 30 days [Follow the MIND diet principles as closely as you can]

Nutrition absolutely matters! *We really are what we eat.* There is overwhelming evidence that supports the vitally important role that good nutrition plays in both physical and mental health.

Log Your Meals/Snacks/Beverages/Alcohol

The only thing you are required to do to successfully meet the program expectations for Nutrition is to log everything you eat and drink. When we say everything, that's exactly what we mean - your meals, snacks, and beverages, including alcohol. You may decide to keep an electronic log, or you may want to use a paper diary. Either option is fine.

If you choose to keep an electronic log, there are many food diary apps available. The one we recommend is a free smartphone app called MyFitnessPal (www.MyFitnessPal.com). If you're already using a food diary app to log your food, please feel free to continue using that app. If you don't have a smartphone, you can access www.MyFitnessPal.com, or any of the other food diary apps via your computer.

Download the app prior to beginning the program to become familiar with its features. You're welcome to set a caloric intake and a weight loss goal but to satisfy the program expectations, we only ask that you log your intake. The goal is to increase your mindful awareness of what you're consuming.

If you prefer to keep a paper diary, please feel free to do so. Whether you use an app such as MyFitnessPal or a paper diary, this habit of logging will change your behavior for the better, and your mind-body health will benefit. Additionally, the logging generates more mindfulness about food and eating behaviors.

Research has shown that many people who keep a food journal lose weight. There are several explanations for the weight loss. First, when you write down everything you eat and drink, you tend to be much more aware of what you're consuming. The very act of recording everything means that you're no longer engaging in mindless eating, which often results in weight gain. Second, just knowing that you are required to log everything into your food journal can be a deterrent to overeating.

To successfully meet the program expectations for this element, you are required to log your meals, snacks, and beverages, including alcohol. The rest of this chapter contains additional recommendations and resources that we think will enhance your experience. However, these are only recommendations and are not requirements.

> ## Be Mindful of What You're Eating and How Much You're Eating. Mindful Awareness is at the Heart of this Element!

Additional Program Recommendations and Resources

1. MIND diet

The MIND diet was created by Martha Clare Morris, PhD, a nutritional epidemiologist and her colleagues at Rush University Medical Center, and it is based on many years of research concerning brain function and diet. The MIND diet is a hybrid of the Mediterranean and DASH (Dietary Approaches to Stop Hypertension) diets. MIND stands for Mediterranean-DASH Intervention for Neurodegenerative Delay. *U.S. News & World Report* has issued an annual "Best Diets" list, ranking 35 different diets. In 2016, the MIND diet tied for first in the *'easiest diet to follow'* category and tied for second in the *'best overall diet'* category. Recent research has shown that people who followed the diet faithfully reduced their risk of developing Alzheimer's Disease by up to 53 percent, and those who followed the MIND diet reasonably well, reduced their risk of developing Alzheimer's by 35%.

The MIND diet follows the Mediterranean diet principles of eating more vegetables, fruits, whole grains, fish, olive oil, and nuts. Those following the diet are asked to minimize or eliminate red meats, processed meats, and simple and refined carbohydrates such as flour, bread, pastries, and sugar.

We *strongly* recommend that you incorporate the MIND diet principles into your nutritional plan because it has shown very impressive pro-brain and pro-mental health benefits. Given these positive scientific findings, please do your best to adopt the MIND diet way of eating.

The MIND diet recommendations are outlined in the graphic on the next page. To learn even more about the MIND diet, and to access 42 MIND diet recipes go to www.bebrainfit.com/mind-diet-recipes.

If you're vegan or vegetarian, we are not asking you to change your eating habits to include protein from animal sources. Simply incorporate the elements of the MIND diet that fit your current vegan/vegetarian lifestyle. The MIND diet does not provide recommendations regarding eggs.

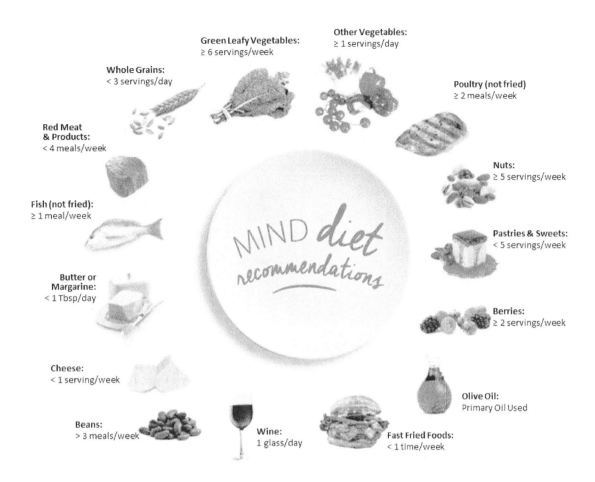

Green Leafy Vegetables:
≥ 6 servings/week

Other Vegetables:
≥ 1 servings/day

Whole Grains:
< 3 servings/day

Poultry (not fried)
≥ 2 meals/week

Red Meat
& Products:
< 4 meals/week

Nuts:
≥ 5 servings/week

Fish (not fried):
≥ 1 meal/week

Pastries & Sweets:
< 5 servings/week

Butter or
Margarine:
< 1 Tbsp/day

Berries:
≥ 2 servings/week

Cheese:
< 1 serving/week

Olive Oil:
Primary Oil Used

Beans:
> 3 meals/week

Wine:
1 glass/day

Fast Fried Foods:
< 1 time/week

MIND diet recommendations

Due to inflammation concerns, the MIND diet limits the consumption of dairy. Both cheese and butter recommendations are noted on the chart. However, recommendations for yogurt are not included. Do your best to minimize dairy consumption. If you do not drink alcohol, if you're in recovery, or under age, please disregard the recommendation to drink one glass of wine per day!

2. Mindful Moment with a Raisin

If you're new to the practice of mindful eating, we suggest you listen to the *Mindful Moment with a Raisin* exercise. This recording is a free download available at **www.wild5meditations.com**. This meditation provides an excellent introduction to the practice of mindful eating.

3. Mindful Meal Meditation

If you decide to explore mindful eating practices further, this exercise is an option you may want to consider. To better understand the practice of mindful eating, please listen to the *Introduction to Mindful Meal Meditation* once, before using the *Mindful Meal Meditation.* You may divide the exercise into two 10-minute segments listening to it during two meals/snacks a day. These recordings are free downloads and can be found at **www.wild5meditations.com.**

> **REMEMBER: While we strongly recommend that you follow the MIND diet, given its pro-brain and pro-mental health benefits, this is only a recommendation and not a program requirement.**

FAQs

1. Why is food logging so important to my mental wellness?

Every single chemical and neurotransmitter in your brain is created from FOOD! Yes, we are indeed what we eat! If you eat poorly, both your mind and your body suffer. One more thing to remember, excess calories lead to poor brain health. By logging your food regularly, using an app such as MyFitnessPal or a paper diary, you will become more aware of what you eat, and hopefully, based on this increased mindful awareness, you'll make changes that ultimately benefit your body, brain, and mental wellness. Logging is crucial!

2. What is the MIND diet? Why is it being recommended for LiveWell90?

The MIND diet is a research-based way of eating that has been shown to protect both your brain and body. The diet is easy to follow and emphasizes plant-based nutrition, with limited amounts of animal proteins. This is a simple and effective way to improve your global health and wellbeing without too much effort.

3. Is MyFitnessPal an easy app or website to use?

Yes, it is! The app is highly educational and motivational in nature and does a great job of increasing your overall mindful awareness of what you're consuming. Please download the app to your smartphone prior to starting the program and become familiar with its features. This app motivates users to eat better. If you're not a fan of apps, keep a paper food diary. If you're already using another food logging app, like Weight Watchers, there is no need to change.

4. Can I follow the MIND diet for a lifetime?

Absolutely! This diet should be followed for years to gain maximum benefit. It's rich in good fats and limits bad fats (from animal sources), plus it encourages you to eat nuts, vegetables, and fruits. It's a win-win lifestyle modification that pays off very handsomely in many ways.

5. Is LiveWell90 a weight loss program?

No, LiveWell90 was not created to be a weight loss program. However, there is scientific evidence showing that many people who write down everything they eat and drink on a regular basis, do in fact lose weight. Keeping a food diary significantly reduces mindless eating which can be a major factor in gaining weight.

Barriers to Success

Below are a few potential barriers along with suggested solutions:

Time – Take the time to log your meals/snacks/beverages/alcohol throughout the day. Try your best to avoid waiting until bedtime to complete your log. Keep up the practice - it will get easier as you go along. We suggest adding a reminder to log your intake to your calendar and set reminder alerts to increase the chances of meeting your goals.

Low Motivation – Acknowledge your lack of drive/motivation as a common feeling when starting the practice of keeping a food log, implementing a new meal plan, and/or practicing mindful eating. On days when you don't feel like doing these activities, do them anyway - no matter what! A couple of other suggestions:

1. Consider enlisting the help of an accountability buddy; someone you'll alert each day letting them know you've completed your wellness practices, and

2. Consider practicing the *5 Second Rule* on days when you're experiencing low motivation (see *Tackling Low Motivation* on page 47 for information about the *5 Second Rule*).

Words of Advice

*Perfection is **NOT** the goal! Set your goals high and do your best every day. Be kind to yourself as you begin making these changes. Change is never easy. If you miss a day or two, shake it off, regroup, and begin again. Do not throw in the towel. Remember to track your nutrition practices using the Participant Tracking Form (page 55).*

What Others are Saying

"I have already lost weight. I'm developing a new appreciation of the taste of food. I feel very strongly that the "mindful eating meditation" is integral to success with changing eating habits. It slows everything down, maintains awareness, enhances the appreciation of food, and interestingly, when done appropriately it cuts down the amount of food I even want completely outside of my conscious awareness."

~DH

"I have lost ten pounds since the completion of the survey. It has helped me feel better about myself. This program has helped to show me that with a bit more attention to what I'm eating and some exercise, I can change my body for the better. I never ate terribly, but the amount of sugar and caffeine I was using to keep going took a toll. I feel better about what I'm eating and I'm happier that I am more active."

~KB

HERO WELLNESS SCALE

It will be important for you to know if your LiveWell90 efforts are resulting in actual improvements. There's a famous saying from the world of business that explains why measurement matters — *You can't manage what you don't measure*. To improve your wellness, you **must** measure it.

The *HERO Wellness Scale* is a validated wellness instrument that is designed to measure wellness changes. This measurement tool is your guide to better understanding how your wellness is improving as a result of participating in LiveWell90. Keeping an eye on your wellness status throughout the 90-day program can also serve as a source of motivation.

The *HERO Wellness Scale* asks you to rate your happiness, enthusiasm, resilience, optimism, and mental wellness for the previous seven days, using a scale ranging from 0-10 (0=lowest score and 10=highest score).

In total, you will complete the *HERO Wellness Scale* four times during the program. Copies of the *HERO Wellness Scale* are located in the workbook. We've included a copy on the following page so that you can familiarize yourself with the scale and its layout.

We recommend you use the *HERO Wellness Scale* to track the results of your wellness practices during the 90-day program. Once you complete the program, you can access copies of the *HERO Wellness Scale* at www.WILD5Wellness.com/forms.

HERO WELLNESS SCALE

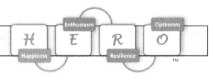

*Please circle **ONE NUMBER** for each question below.*

1. On average, during the last 7 DAYS, how happy have you felt?

0	1	2	3	4	5	6	7	8	9	10
Not at all happy		Mildly happy			Moderately happy			Highly happy		Extremely happy

2. On average, during the last 7 DAYS, how enthusiastic have you felt?

0	1	2	3	4	5	6	7	8	9	10
Not at all enthusiastic		Mildly enthusiastic		Moderately enthusiastic				Highly enthusiastic		Extremely enthusiastic

3. On average, during the last 7 DAYS, how resilient have you felt?

0	1	2	3	4	5	6	7	8	9	10
Not at all resilient		Mildly resilient			Moderately resilient			Highly resilient		Extremely resilient

4. On average, during the last 7 DAYS, how optimistic have you felt?

0	1	2	3	4	5	6	7	8	9	10
Not at all optimistic	Mildly optimistic			Moderately optimistic			Highly optimistic			Extremely optimistic

5. On average, during the last 7 DAYS, how would you rate your mental wellness?

0	1	2	3	4	5	6	7	8	9	10
Not at all good		Mildly good			Moderately good			Markedly good		Extremely good

- -

SCORING: To calculate total score, add all circled numbers.

TOTAL SCORE: 0 - 50

HIGHER SCORES INDICATE HIGHER LEVELS OF WELLNESS

SCORE

© Copyright 2019 Saundra Jain & Rakesh Jain. All Rights Reserved.

WHY HERO EXERCISES MATTER

Do you have any heroes – people you admire that have positively influenced your life? Most of us report having heroes, but what about your own internal HERO? What is that, you may ask? Well, we've created an acronym, **HERO,** to represent our internal HERO, which stands for **H**appiness, **E**nthusiasm, **R**esilience, and **O**ptimism.

It's remarkable how each of the HERO wellness traits - happiness, enthusiasm, resilience, and optimism – positively impact overall wellness. HERO is:

- Linked to longevity
- Linked to a stronger immune system
- Mitigates pain
- Predicts lower heart rate and blood pressure
- Predicts lower rates of depression
- Linked to better physical wellbeing
- Linked to better coping skills

Given these benefits, spending about 5 minutes a day strengthening your internal HERO makes sense. Because the power of these exercises is so convincing, we'd like to share the findings from a recent WILD 5 Wellness research poster presented at a national mental health meeting (Jain S, Jain R. Poster presentation at: 29th Annual US Psychiatric and Mental Health Congress; October 2016; San Antonio, Texas). The improvements noted below occurred after a 30-day WILD 5 Wellness intervention:

- Happiness scores improved by 30%
- Enthusiasm scores improved by 51%
- Resilience scores improved by 63%
- Optimism scores improved by 45%

As you can see, investing the time to complete the HERO exercises, makes a big difference in the four HERO wellness traits. It's possible to strengthen your internal HERO in a very short period of time.

The HERO exercises are in addition to the LiveWell90 practices of exercise, mindfulness, sleep, social connectedness, and nutrition. This may sound like a lot of work but remember the HERO exercises only take 5 minutes a day, and they are well-worth the time and effort.

To get the most out of your HERO exercises, it's important to take the time to review your previously answered HERO questions. We promise you that this is not busy work – there are incredible mental health benefits associated with reviewing and reminding yourself of previous thoughts and successes. During your review, ask yourself if you are noticing any patterns. Do you see any areas where you're struggling? Are you observing any positive changes?

As you work through these exercises, you will notice the questions are recycled every eight days. There is a reason for the repetition – let us explain. Throughout the program, we want you to periodically review your answers to the HERO questions. This repetitive, reflective review increases your mindful awareness, which in turn strengthens your internal HERO.

As you begin these exercises, you'll notice there is some overlap between the HERO wellness traits. For example, happy people are often more enthusiastic, resilient, and optimistic. Strengthening one of the HERO wellness traits, helps enhance the others.

Barriers to Success

This is a new activity, so remembering to do these exercises may be a challenge for some. Below are a few potential barriers along with suggested solutions:

- **Time** – Find a time that works best for you to complete the HERO exercises. We suggest adding this activity to your calendar and set reminder alerts to increase the chances of meeting your goals.

- **Low Motivation** – Acknowledge your lack of drive/motivation as a common feeling when deciding to do the HERO exercises. On days when you don't feel like doing your HERO exercises, do them anyway - no matter what! A couple of other suggestions:

  1. Consider enlisting the help of an accountability buddy; someone you'll alert each day letting them know you've completed your wellness practices, and

  2. Consider practicing the *5 Second Rule* on days when you're experiencing low motivation (see Tackling Low Motivation on page 47 for information about the *5 Second Rule*).

As you establish this practice, you will come to value this time of thoughtful reflection. Please don't underestimate the power of these exercises. Each of the HERO wellness traits - happiness, enthusiasm, resilience, and optimism – can be strengthened by completing the exercises.

What Others are Saying

"The HERO exercises helped me refocus my thoughts and find positive things in my life to focus on rather than negative thoughts that filled my mind more often before WILD 5. Before I started the program, I had a difficult time finding the positive in my day, but now I see the positive things in my life and feel more thankful for what I have and the people I have in my life."

~ KV

WHY PREPARATION MATTERS

As you prepare to begin LiveWell90, remember this: A little preparation goes a long way! We understand that you're eager to get started, but please take the time to review the checklist below, allowing yourself plenty of time (3 to 5 days) to review and complete these items prior to beginning the program.

Most people say they decided to do the program because they wanted to feel better and improve their overall sense of wellness. What are your reasons for doing this program? Let's not stop with this question. Let's go one step further – what are you willing to give up so you can achieve your goals? This question is the result of several conversations with our colleague and friend, Dr. Christine Whelan, Clinical Professor, Department of Consumer Science, School of Human Ecology at The University of Wisconsin in Madison. While discussing the program, she asked us what we thought participants were willing to give up so they could achieve their goals. A light bulb went off for both of us as we realized we needed to ask participants this question to increase the likelihood they would achieve their goals. Many thanks to Dr. Whelan for opening our eyes to this powerful question.

If you're going to make this kind of wellness commitment, one that requires time, dedication, patience, persistence, and determination, then why not take the time to answer these two questions?

1. **Why do you want to do LiveWell90?**

   _____
   _____
   _____

2. **What are you willing to give up to ensure that your LiveWell90 experience is successful?**

   _____
   _____
   _____

Please don't rush through this section. Take some time and consider these two questions, as both require thought and reflection. The more effort you put into answering these two questions, the better your chances of getting the most out of the program.

If you want to fully commit to this program to achieve your goals, this requires some sacrifices. For example, you may have to:

- Sacrifice dinner with friends to get your workout completed
- Sacrifice your favorite television show to meet the program expectations for sleep

- Tolerate family and friends teasing you about mindfully meditating

You may encounter many sacrifices during this 90-day program. Are you willing to make those sacrifices to achieve your goals?

Let's now turn our attention to the items listed below. Do your best to give this list the time and attention it deserves. We assure you that all the front-end preparation will pay off!

PREPARATION TO-DO LIST
PRIOR TO YOUR START DATE PLEASE CHECK OFF EACH ITEM AS COMPLETED

- ☐ Consult with your healthcare provider before beginning this program.
- ☐ Review your LiveWell90 workbook cover-to-cover, making sure you fully understand the program.
- ☐ Select an accountability buddy, if you've decided to use one.
- ☐ Inform friend(s)/family member(s) about participation in the program to gain their support and encouragement.
- ☐ Review options as to type of exercise and time of day for exercise. You may want to consider putting your exercise plan on your calendar with reminder alerts.
- ☐ Select a workout buddy, if you've decided to use one.
- ☐ Make sure you have a good pair of walking/running shoes.
- ☐ Review the mindfulness meditation options – consider the WILD 5 Wellness guided meditations if you're new to meditating. If you're a more seasoned meditator, consider one of the many mindfulness meditation apps currently available. Make these decisions prior to starting the program. Give yourself plenty of time to make this decision. Listen to the different meditations and decide which is best, based on your needs and personal preference.
- ☐ The WILD 5 Mindfulness Meditations are available online at:

www.WILD5meditations.com

You may download these meditations to your smartphone, computer, tablet, or you may play them on your computer.

- ☐ Decide on the time and location for your mindfulness practice. You may want to consider putting this on your calendar with reminder alerts.
- ☐ Decide on the sitting equipment you'll be using when meditating - chair, firm cushion or meditation bench.
- ☐ Consider ways to eliminate all ambient light in your bedroom, i.e. blackout shades and/or sleep mask.
- ☐ Decide on your bedtime. You may want to consider putting this on your calendar with reminder alerts.

☐ Make a list of ways you want to connect with others. You may want to consider putting these events on your calendar with reminder alerts.

☐ If using a smartphone app to log your food, download the app and become familiar with its features.

☐ Review the MIND diet recommendations, making sure your pantry is adequately stocked with brain-healthy foods.

☐ Clear your kitchen of all unhealthy processed foods to avoid temptations.

☐ Decide when you will complete your *Daily Journaling Form* and your HERO exercises (pages 61-63). You may want to consider putting these on your calendar with reminder alerts.

☐ Review the *Participant Tracking Form* (page 55). You may want to consider putting a reminder alert on your calendar to make sure you remember to track your practices.

☐ Complete the *HERO Wellness Scale* (pages 57-59) prior to your start date.

TACKLING LOW MOTIVATION

A potential barrier to meeting program expectations is low motivation. There will be days when you know you should do your LiveWell90 practices, but you don't feel like it, and you may end up skipping one or more. Mel Robbins' bestselling book, *The 5 Second Rule*, offers an effective strategy for dealing with times when you don't feel like doing your LiveWell90 practices. We want to share some of her ideas.

Many of us are resistant to doing anything new if it feels difficult. We all have things we want to do, or know we should do, yet we don't do them. According to Robbins, if we hesitate to act, we give our brains time to come up with excuses to avoid action.

As an example, you decide to set your alarm 15 minutes earlier because you plan to do your 10-minute mindfulness meditation practice as soon as you wake up. Your alarm goes off, and your initial response is to hit the snooze button, rather than doing your meditation. The longer you wait between the impulse to act, which in this example is getting out of bed when you hear the alarm, the less likely you are to meditate. According to Robbins, when you get the impulse to work on your goal, you must take the first physical step toward achieving the goal within five seconds, or your mind will talk you out of doing it. This is what is known as the *five second rule*.

As soon as you feel any hesitation to act, Robbins recommends counting backwards from 5 - 5 4 3 2 1 - and when you get to 1, you immediately take action toward accomplishing your goal. This approach allows you to act before your mind sabotages you with doubts, fears, and excuses. In the example, as soon as you begin thinking about not getting out of bed to meditate, you begin to count backwards from 5. When you reach 1, you get out of bed and begin preparing to do your 10-minute mindfulness meditation.

Feelings often factor into our decision-making process. When deciding to do something, it's not really a matter of wanting to do it, but rather whether we feel like doing it. Feelings favor whatever feels good or is easiest, and not what is in our best interest. If you act only when you feel like it, you'll never get what you desire. You must separate how you feel from the actions you need to take. The *five second rule* is designed to help you do this.

There may be days when you won't feel like doing a LiveWell90 practice. You'll think of reasons to skip the practice. The moment you realize that you're thinking about whether you feel like doing your practice, count backwards from 5, and when you reach 1, take action. When you do this regularly, successfully completing the program expectations will become routine.

Find out more about Mel Robbins and her book, *The 5 Second Rule* at www.melrobbins.com.

WHY TRACKING MATTERS

We cannot overestimate the importance of regular tracking. Sticking to the program isn't always easy - you may encounter challenges and barriers along the way. Despite these challenges and barriers, making true lifestyle changes requires consistent practice.

I'm a Type I diabetic (this is Saundra, by the way) and tracking my blood sugars matters. If asked what my blood sugars were last Tuesday, your guess is as good as mine - I'd have no idea. However, good record keeping allows me to accurately retrieve that information. Plus, I can look at trends in my blood sugars and better understand where and why I'm experiencing problems. The same is true for these wellness practices – tracking matters!

To help you develop sustainable changes, we ask you to document your LiveWell90 practices as follows:

- **Paper Copy:** Your workbook includes a *Participant Tracking Form* (page 55). A downloadable copy is available at www.WILD5Wellness.com/forms for you to continue tracking your wellness practices once you complete the 90-day program. Reviewing your wellness practices for patterns or trends will help you better understand how you're doing. Based on your findings, you can proactively adjust your schedule or set reminder alerts to improve your program participation. Make the *Participant Tracking Form* work for you! The information this form contains is valuable and will help you stick with the program.

- **Daily Journaling:** This form, also located in your workbook, allows you to track other information about your LiveWell90 practices. As an example, there's a place to document which guided meditation(s) you used that day, the type, duration, and intensity of your exercise, whether you practiced a mindful meal meditation, and a place to document your barriers and solutions. We strongly recommend that you take the time to complete the *Daily Journaling Form* (page 62), so you can capture useful information about your wellness practices. Based on this information, you can proactively adjust your schedule or set reminder alerts to improve your program participation. A downloadable copy of the *Daily Journaling Form* is available at www.WILD5Wellness.com/forms, which allows you to continue tracking your wellness practices once you complete the 90-day program.

We recommend you find someone to be your accountability buddy. Research shows that being accountable to another person can be very helpful in accomplishing goals. Let your buddy know that you've decided to increase your own personal wellness by participating in LiveWell90. Tell them that you'll be checking in with them to let them know if you've met your wellness goals. In addition to helping you stay on track with your wellness practices, an accountability buddy also provides you with increased social connection and positive reinforcement for all the work you're doing. We strongly encourage you to build in a true point of accountability before beginning the program, by making this important connection with another person.

In fact, you may want to recruit a wellness buddy to do LiveWell90 with you. We've had several people recruit friends, family members, spouses, partners, and co-workers to join them in this wellness program. This appears to be a great way to improve personal accountability.

YOUR LIVEWELL90 JOURNEY BEGINS

LiveWell90 will provide you with detailed information about how to increase your mental wellness. The program expectations are straightforward and specific.

Participants often want to negotiate which of the program components they're willing to do. For example, they will agree by saying, "I like most of the components, but I don't want to log everything I eat and drink. Can I do the other parts of the program and leave out the nutrition piece?" The answer is no. *There's no room for negotiation*. To fully reap the benefits of LiveWell90, it's important that you commit to working on all components of the program. We understand that completing all program expectations can be challenging. There may be days when you're not able to complete everything, or days when you forget because your schedule is hijacked by life's demands. Whatever the reason, keep in mind that *perfection is not the goal*. If you end up off course, don't worry about it. Shake it off and begin again.

With your copy of the LiveWell90 workbook in hand, it's time to get started! The workbook contains everything you'll need to complete the program. Now, it's time to:

- Complete the *Preparation To-Do List* (pages 44-45)
- Complete the *HERO Wellness Scale* – Day 1 (pages 57-59)
- Set your start date (record below), and
- Start achieving your wellness goals

We recognize that your participation in LiveWell90 requires a considerable commitment on your part, both in terms of time and in learning to incorporate new behaviors into your life. However, based on our research, the wellness benefits you'll receive from participating in the program far outweigh the sacrifices you'll be making.

WELCOME! Congratulations on making
a *commitment* to your personal *wellness*!

MY START DATE:

Phase 1

START

- Program Expectations
- Participant Tracking Form
- HERO Wellness Scale (Day 1)
- Daily Journaling & HERO Exercises
- HERO Wellness Scale (Day 30)

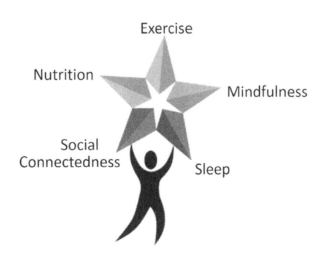

WILD 5☆ Wellness®
Wellness Interventions for Life's Demands

Phase 1
START

PROGRAM EXPECTATIONS

Exercise	Exercise 30 minutes <u>each day</u> for 30 days, aim for at least moderate intensity*
Mindfulness	Practice mindfulness for at least 10 minutes <u>each day</u> for 30 days
Sleep	Implement 4 or more of the 6 sleep hygiene practices <u>each day</u> for 30 days
Social Connectedness	Meet or call a minimum of two friends or family members <u>each day</u> for 30 days
Nutrition	Log your meals/snacks/beverages/alcohol <u>each day</u> for 30 days [Follow the MIND diet principles as closely as you can]

* *Consult your healthcare provider before starting any exercise program. If you're unable to reach 30 minutes of exercise per day or reach moderate intensity as you begin the program that is fine. Do whatever you're capable of doing. Base the amount of time you exercise and the intensity of your exercise on your physical capabilities.*

WILD 5⭐ Wellness™

Wellness Interventions for Life's Demands

LiveWell90

Participant Tracking Form

Phase 1: START

Start Date: _____

	Exercise — Did I exercise today following the FID principles?		Mindfulness — Did I mindfully meditate at least 10 minutes today?		Sleep — Did I implement 4 or more of the 6 sleep hygiene practices?		Connectedness — Did I socially connect with at least 2 people today?		Nutrition — Did I log my meals, snacks, and beverages, including alcohol today?		HERO — Did I complete my HERO exercises today?	
	YES	NO	YES	NO	YES	NO	YES	NO	YES	NO	YES	NO
1	○	○	○	○	○	○	○	○	○	○	○	○
2	○	○	○	○	○	○	○	○	○	○	○	○
3	○	○	○	○	○	○	○	○	○	○	○	○
4	○	○	○	○	○	○	○	○	○	○	○	○
5	○	○	○	○	○	○	○	○	○	○	○	○
6	○	○	○	○	○	○	○	○	○	○	○	○
7	○	○	○	○	○	○	○	○	○	○	○	○
8	○	○	○	○	○	○	○	○	○	○	○	○
9	○	○	○	○	○	○	○	○	○	○	○	○
10	○	○	○	○	○	○	○	○	○	○	○	○
11	○	○	○	○	○	○	○	○	○	○	○	○
12	○	○	○	○	○	○	○	○	○	○	○	○
13	○	○	○	○	○	○	○	○	○	○	○	○
14	○	○	○	○	○	○	○	○	○	○	○	○
15	○	○	○	○	○	○	○	○	○	○	○	○
	YES	NO	YES	NO	YES	NO	YES	NO	YES	NO	YES	NO

© Copyright 2019 Saundra Jain & Rakesh Jain. All Rights Reserved.

Day	Exercise Did I exercise today following the FID principles?		Mindfulness Did I mindfully meditate at least 10 minutes today?		Sleep Did I implement 4 or more of the 6 sleep hygiene practices?		Connectedness Did I socially connect with at least 2 people today?		Nutrition Did I log my meals, snacks, and beverages, including alcohol today?		HERO Did I complete my HERO exercises today?	
	YES	NO	YES	NO	YES	NO	YES	NO	YES	NO	YES	NO
16	○	○	○	○	○	○	○	○	○	○	○	○
17	○	○	○	○	○	○	○	○	○	○	○	○
18	○	○	○	○	○	○	○	○	○	○	○	○
19	○	○	○	○	○	○	○	○	○	○	○	○
20	○	○	○	○	○	○	○	○	○	○	○	○
21	○	○	○	○	○	○	○	○	○	○	○	○
22	○	○	○	○	○	○	○	○	○	○	○	○
23	○	○	○	○	○	○	○	○	○	○	○	○
24	○	○	○	○	○	○	○	○	○	○	○	○
25	○	○	○	○	○	○	○	○	○	○	○	○
26	○	○	○	○	○	○	○	○	○	○	○	○
27	○	○	○	○	○	○	○	○	○	○	○	○
28	○	○	○	○	○	○	○	○	○	○	○	○
29	○	○	○	○	○	○	○	○	○	○	○	○
30	○	○	○	○	○	○	○	○	○	○	○	○

© Copyright 2019 Saundra Jain & Rakesh Jain. All Rights Reserved.

56

HERO Wellness Scale

Day 1

Please complete the *HERO Wellness Scale* on the next page before you begin the program. This scale is your way to measure and track your wellness throughout the program. Please don't underestimate the value of using the *HERO Wellness Scale*, as the feedback will be both useful and motivational.

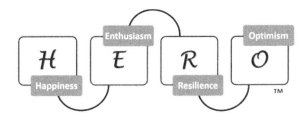

HERO WELLNESS SCALE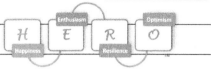

*Please circle **ONE NUMBER** for each question below.*

1. On average, during the last 7 DAYS, how happy have you felt?

0	1	2	3	4	5	6	7	8	9	10

Not at all happy   Mildly happy   Moderately happy   Highly happy   Extremely happy

2. On average, during the last 7 DAYS, how enthusiastic have you felt?

0	1	2	3	4	5	6	7	8	9	10

Not at all enthusiastic   Mildly enthusiastic   Moderately enthusiastic   Highly enthusiastic   Extremely enthusiastic

3. On average, during the last 7 DAYS, how resilient have you felt?

0	1	2	3	4	5	6	7	8	9	10

Not at all resilient   Mildly resilient   Moderately resilient   Highly resilient   Extremely resilient

4. On average, during the last 7 DAYS, how optimistic have you felt?

0	1	2	3	4	5	6	7	8	9	10

Not at all optimistic   Mildly optimistic   Moderately optimistic   Highly optimistic   Extremely optimistic

5. On average, during the last 7 DAYS, how would you rate your mental wellness?

0	1	2	3	4	5	6	7	8	9	10

Not at all good   Mildly good   Moderately good   Markedly good   Extremely good

---

SCORING: To calculate total score, add all circled numbers.

TOTAL SCORE: 0 - 50

HIGHER SCORES INDICATE HIGHER LEVELS OF WELLNESS

SCORE

WILD 5☆ Wellness®
Wellness Interventions for Life's Demands

© Copyright 2019 Saundra Jain & Rakesh Jain. All Rights Reserved.

Daily Journaling and HERO Exercises

Using the *Daily Journaling Form* allows you to capture useful information on a daily basis about your LiveWell90 wellness practices. It asks you to document what you did each day to meet the program expectations for each of the 5 wellness components. You are also asked to record any barriers you encountered, and the solutions you used to overcome them.

HERO exercises are designed to improve your mental wellness. Doing them daily increases and enriches your levels of happiness, enthusiasm, resilience, and optimism.

Daily Journaling Form

EXERCISE	Exercise 30 minutes each day for 30 days, aim for at least moderate intensity		
Type of Exercise		Duration	_____ minutes
Intensity	☐ Low	☐ Moderate	☐ High

MINDFULNESS	Practice mindfulness at least 10 minutes each day for 30 days
Today's Guided Meditation(s)	

SLEEP	Implement 4 or more of the 6 sleep hygiene practices each day for 30 days		
Implemented These Sleep Hygiene Practices	☐ No electronics 90 min before bed	☐ Sleep mask or blackout shades	☐ Regular bedtime
	☐ No napping	☐ Warm bath/shower prior to bed	☐ Avoid caffeine 10 hrs before bed

SOCIAL CONNECTEDNESS	Meet or call at least two friends or family members each day for 30 days			
	Friends		**Family**	
Today's Social Contacts	☐ Call	☐ In-person	☐ Call	☐ In-person

NUTRITION	Log your daily meals/snacks/beverages/alcohol each day for 30 days	
Logged Meals/Snacks/Beverages/Alcohol	☐ Yes	☐ No
Strongly Recommended		
Implemented MIND Diet Principles	☐ Yes	☐ No
Practiced Mindful Meal Meditation	☐ Breakfast ☐ Lunch ☐ Dinner	

TODAY'S PROGRESS	
My Barrier(s)	
My Solution(s)	

HERO Exercises
Happiness • Enthusiasm • Resilience • Optimism

HERO

HAPPINESS & ENTHUSIASM ARE LINKED TO LONGEVITY

1. To increase your happiness, let's work on strengthening your happiness muscle. Take a moment and write down two positive things that you'd like to experience today. Also, two to three times today, find a few minutes to visualize and relish these positive experiences.

   a. _____

   _____

   b. _____

   _____

2. Having a goal or a project that inspires you will increase your enthusiasm. Write down two projects you find inspiring and set a start date. Put the date on your calendar with reminder alerts – make it happen and watch your enthusiasm improve!

   a. _____

   _____

   b. _____

   _____

The HERO exercises are intentionally repeated every 8 days because repetition is crucial to learning and incorporating new ideas. After today, review your previous HERO exercises, as research shows that reflecting on past thoughts about wellness further strengthens and solidifies your HERO wellness traits.

Enthusiasm moves the world.
~ Arthur Balfour

Daily Journaling Form

EXERCISE	Exercise 30 minutes each day for 30 days, aim for at least moderate intensity		
Type of Exercise		**Duration**	_____ minutes
Intensity	☐ Low	☐ Moderate	☐ High

MINDFULNESS	Practice mindfulness at least 10 minutes each day for 30 days
Today's Guided Meditation(s)	

SLEEP	Implement 4 or more of the 6 sleep hygiene practices each day for 30 days		
Implemented These Sleep Hygiene Practices	☐ No electronics 90 min before bed	☐ Sleep mask or blackout shades	☐ Regular bedtime
	☐ No napping	☐ Warm bath/shower prior to bed	☐ Avoid caffeine 10 hrs before bed

SOCIAL CONNECTEDNESS	Meet or call at least two friends or family members each day for 30 days			
	Friends		**Family**	
Today's Social Contacts	☐ Call	☐ In-person	☐ Call	☐ In-person

NUTRITION	Log your daily meals/snacks/beverages/alcohol each day for 30 days	
Logged Meals/Snacks/Beverages/Alcohol	☐ Yes	☐ No
Strongly Recommended		
Implemented MIND Diet Principles	☐ Yes	☐ No
Practiced Mindful Meal Meditation	☐ Breakfast ☐ Lunch ☐ Dinner	

TODAY'S PROGRESS	
My Barrier(s)	
My Solution(s)	

HERO Exercises
*H*appiness • *E*nthusiasm • *R*esilience • *O*ptimism

RESILIENT OPTIMISTS HAVE BETTER PHYSICAL HEALTH & BETTER RELATIONSHIPS

1. Resilience means the ability to bounce back from adversities. Write down 2 things about yourself that make you tough, and two skills you have used previously to overcome adversities. Remind yourself throughout the day that you genuinely possess these resilient traits.

   a. _____

   _____

   b. _____

   _____

2. Optimism often requires making a choice about how you view the world. Write down two positive things you want to happen tomorrow, and then spend a few minutes planning on how to make these optimistic attitudes/events a reality.

   a. _____

   _____

   b. _____

   _____

Please take time to review your previous HERO exercises. Research shows that reflecting on past thoughts about wellness further strengthens and solidifies your HERO wellness traits. The HERO exercises are intentionally repeated every 8 days because repetition is crucial to learning and incorporating new ideas.

Choose to be optimistic, it feels better.
~ Dalai Lama XIV

Daily Journaling Form

EXERCISE	Exercise 30 minutes each day for 30 days, aim for at least moderate intensity		
Type of Exercise		Duration	_____ minutes
Intensity	☐ Low	☐ Moderate	☐ High

MINDFULNESS	Practice mindfulness at least 10 minutes each day for 30 days
Today's Guided Meditation(s)	

SLEEP	Implement 4 or more of the 6 sleep hygiene practices each day for 30 days		
Implemented These Sleep Hygiene Practices	☐ No electronics 90 min before bed	☐ Sleep mask or blackout shades	☐ Regular bedtime
	☐ No napping	☐ Warm bath/shower prior to bed	☐ Avoid caffeine 10 hrs before bed

SOCIAL CONNECTEDNESS	Meet or call at least two friends or family members each day for 30 days			
	Friends		Family	
Today's Social Contacts	☐ Call	☐ In-person	☐ Call	☐ In-person

NUTRITION	Log your daily meals/snacks/beverages/ alcohol each day for 30 days	
Logged Meals/Snacks/Beverages/Alcohol	☐ Yes	☐ No
Strongly Recommended		
Implemented MIND Diet Principles	☐ Yes	☐ No
Practiced Mindful Meal Meditation	☐ Breakfast ☐ Lunch ☐ Dinner	

TODAY'S PROGRESS	
My Barrier(s)	
My Solution(s)	

HERO Exercises
Happiness • Enthusiasm • Resilience • Optimism

HAPPINESS & ENTHUSIASM ARE LINKED TO A STRONGER IMMUNE SYSTEM

1. In today's busy world, it's easy to overlook things that make us happy. Fast-paced lifestyles often become a barrier. Take a moment and mindfully reflect on your day, and write down two things that brought you happiness.

    a. _____

    _____

    b. _____

    _____

2. "Birds of a feather flock together," so surround yourself with happy and enthusiastic people. Write down the names of two people in your life that are happy and enthusiastic. Now, write down how and when you will connect with them.

    a. _____

    _____

    b. _____

    _____

Please take time to review your previous HERO exercises. Research shows that reflecting on past thoughts about wellness further strengthens and solidifies your HERO wellness traits. The HERO exercises are intentionally repeated every 8 days because repetition is crucial to learning and incorporating new ideas.

Enthusiasm is contagious. You want to be a carrier.
~ *Susan Rabin*

Daily Journaling Form

EXERCISE	Exercise 30 minutes each day for 30 days, aim for at least moderate intensity	
Type of Exercise		Duration _____ minutes
Intensity	☐ Low ☐ Moderate ☐ High	

MINDFULNESS	Practice mindfulness at least 10 minutes each day for 30 days
Today's Guided Meditation(s)	

SLEEP	Implement 4 or more of the 6 sleep hygiene practices each day for 30 days		
Implemented These Sleep Hygiene Practices	☐ No electronics 90 min before bed	☐ Sleep mask or blackout shades	☐ Regular bedtime
	☐ No napping	☐ Warm bath/shower prior to bed	☐ Avoid caffeine 10 hrs before bed

SOCIAL CONNECTEDNESS	Meet or call at least two friends or family members each day for 30 days			
	Friends		**Family**	
Today's Social Contacts	☐ Call	☐ In-person	☐ Call	☐ In-person

NUTRITION	Log your daily meals/snacks/beverages/alcohol each day for 30 days	
Logged Meals/Snacks/Beverages/Alcohol	☐ Yes	☐ No
Strongly Recommended		
Implemented MIND Diet Principles	☐ Yes	☐ No
Practiced Mindful Meal Meditation	☐ Breakfast ☐ Lunch ☐ Dinner	

TODAY'S PROGRESS	
My Barrier(s)	
My Solution(s)	

HERO Exercises
Happiness • Enthusiasm • Resilience • Optimism

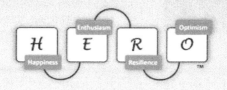

RESILIENT & OPTIMISTIC PEOPLE REPORT BETTER MENTAL HEALTH & LIVE LONGER

1. Dealing with life's challenges with humor builds resilience – the ability to bounce back from life's adversities. Write down two things that happened recently that you found humorous – things that made you smile or laugh.

    a. _____

      _____

    b. _____

      _____

2. Positive affirmations are a great way to build an optimistic mindset. Take a moment and write down two positive statements about yourself, your life, or your future. Purposefully remind yourself of these affirmations several times throughout your day.

    a. _____

      _____

    b. _____

      _____

Please take time to review your previous HERO exercises. Research shows that reflecting on past thoughts about wellness further strengthens and solidifies your HERO wellness traits. The HERO exercises are intentionally repeated every 8 days because repetition is crucial to learning and incorporating new ideas.

Our greatest ally in life is our resilience.
~ Brian Early

Daily Journaling Form

EXERCISE	Exercise 30 minutes each day for 30 days, aim for at least moderate intensity		
Type of Exercise		Duration	_____ minutes
Intensity	☐ Low	☐ Moderate	☐ High

MINDFULNESS	Practice mindfulness at least 10 minutes each day for 30 days
Today's Guided Meditation(s)	

SLEEP	Implement 4 or more of the 6 sleep hygiene practices each day for 30 days		
Implemented These Sleep Hygiene Practices	☐ No electronics 90 min before bed	☐ Sleep mask or blackout shades	☐ Regular bedtime
	☐ No napping	☐ Warm bath/shower prior to bed	☐ Avoid caffeine 10 hrs before bed

SOCIAL CONNECTEDNESS	Meet or call at least two friends or family members each day for 30 days			
	Friends		**Family**	
Today's Social Contacts	☐ Call	☐ In-person	☐ Call	☐ In-person

NUTRITION	Log your daily meals/snacks/beverages/ alcohol each day for 30 days	
Logged Meals/Snacks/Beverages/Alcohol	☐ Yes	☐ No
Strongly Recommended		
Implemented MIND Diet Principles	☐ Yes	☐ No
Practiced Mindful Meal Meditation	☐ Breakfast ☐ Lunch ☐ Dinner	

TODAY'S PROGRESS	
My Barrier(s)	
My Solution(s)	

HERO Exercises
*H*appiness • *E*nthusiasm • *R*esilience • *O*ptimism

HAPPINESS & ENTHUSIASM ARE KNOWN TO LESSEN PAIN

1. Random acts of kindness will increase your happiness! Take a moment and write down two random acts of kindness you will put into action today. If you don't have time to execute your plan today, be sure to make it happen first thing tomorrow morning.

    a. _____

    _____

    b. _____

    _____

2. When it comes to outlook, do you fall on the positive or the negative side of the fence? Having a positive attitude about life improves enthusiasm. To increase your enthusiasm, mindfully consider your day and write down two examples of your positive attitude and/or actions.

    a. _____

    _____

    b. _____

    _____

Please take time to review your previous HERO exercises. Research shows that reflecting on past thoughts about wellness further strengthens and solidifies your HERO wellness traits. The HERO exercises are intentionally repeated every 8 days because repetition is crucial to learning and incorporating new ideas.

Most folks are as happy as they make up their minds to be.
~ Abraham Lincoln

Daily Journaling Form

EXERCISE	Exercise 30 minutes each day for 30 days, aim for at least moderate intensity	
Type of Exercise		Duration _____ minutes
Intensity	☐ Low ☐ Moderate ☐ High	

MINDFULNESS	Practice mindfulness at least 10 minutes each day for 30 days
Today's Guided Meditation(s)	

SLEEP	Implement 4 or more of the 6 sleep hygiene practices each day for 30 days		
Implemented These Sleep Hygiene Practices	☐ No electronics 90 min before bed	☐ Sleep mask or blackout shades	☐ Regular bedtime
	☐ No napping	☐ Warm bath/shower prior to bed	☐ Avoid caffeine 10 hrs before bed

SOCIAL CONNECTEDNESS	Meet or call at least two friends or family members each day for 30 days			
	Friends		**Family**	
Today's Social Contacts	☐ Call	☐ In-person	☐ Call	☐ In-person

NUTRITION	Log your daily meals/snacks/beverages/ alcohol each day for 30 days	
Logged Meals/Snacks/Beverages/Alcohol	☐ Yes	☐ No
Strongly Recommended		
Implemented MIND Diet Principles	☐ Yes	☐ No
Practiced Mindful Meal Meditation	☐ Breakfast ☐ Lunch ☐ Dinner	

TODAY'S PROGRESS	
My Barrier(s)	
My Solution(s)	

HERO Exercises
*H*appiness • *E*nthusiasm • *R*esilience • *O*ptimism

RESILIENCE & OPTIMISM FERTILIZE A POSITIVE ATTITUDE

1. Being of service to others is a great way to build resilience. List two things you did today (or will do tomorrow) to give back to others or to brighten their day.

   a. _____

   _____

   b. _____

   _____

2. Is your glass half-full or half-empty? How you view the world matters! Write down two things that happened today that you viewed as negative. Take a moment and give this some thought, and then write down a less negative, or even a positive interpretation of the same events.

   a. _____

   _____

   b. _____

   _____

Please take time to review your previous HERO exercises. Research shows that reflecting on past thoughts about wellness further strengthens and solidifies your HERO wellness traits. The HERO exercises are intentionally repeated every 8 days because repetition is crucial to learning and incorporating new ideas.

In order to carry a positive action, we must develop here a positive vision.
~ Dalai Lama

Daily Journaling Form

EXERCISE	Exercise 30 minutes each day for 30 days, aim for at least moderate intensity	
Type of Exercise		Duration _____ minutes
Intensity	☐ Low ☐ Moderate ☐ High	

MINDFULNESS	Practice mindfulness at least 10 minutes each day for 30 days
Today's Guided Meditation(s)	

SLEEP	Implement 4 or more of the 6 sleep hygiene practices each day for 30 days		
Implemented These Sleep Hygiene Practices	☐ No electronics 90 min before bed	☐ Sleep mask or blackout shades	☐ Regular bedtime
	☐ No napping	☐ Warm bath/shower prior to bed	☐ Avoid caffeine 10 hrs before bed

SOCIAL CONNECTEDNESS	Meet or call at least two friends or family members each day for 30 days	
Today's Social Contacts	**Friends** ☐ Call ☐ In-person	**Family** ☐ Call ☐ In-person

NUTRITION	Log your daily meals/snacks/beverages/ alcohol each day for 30 days	
Logged Meals/Snacks/Beverages/Alcohol	☐ Yes	☐ No
Strongly Recommended		
Implemented MIND Diet Principles	☐ Yes	☐ No
Practiced Mindful Meal Meditation	☐ Breakfast ☐ Lunch ☐ Dinner	

TODAY'S PROGRESS	
My Barrier(s)	
My Solution(s)	

HERO Exercises
Happiness • Enthusiasm • Resilience • Optimism

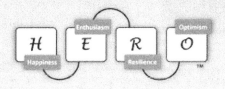

HAPPINESS & ENTHUSIASM PREDICT LOWER HEART RATE & BLOOD PRESSURE

1. Thinking about happy memories can positively impact your level of happiness! Write down two memories that bring a smile to your face. Next, spend a few minutes reliving each of these happy memories, and watch your current level of happiness increase.

   a. _____

   _____

   b. _____

   _____

2. Gratitude is known to increase feelings of happiness and enthusiasm. To increase these feelings, mindfully consider your day and write down two examples of things that happened today that increased your feelings of gratitude.

   a. _____

   _____

   b. _____

   _____

Please take time to review your previous HERO exercises. Research shows that reflecting on past thoughts about wellness further strengthens and solidifies your HERO wellness traits. The HERO exercises are intentionally repeated every 8 days because repetition is crucial to learning and incorporating new ideas.

The worst bankruptcy in the world is the person who has lost his enthusiasm.
~ H.W. Arnold

Daily Journaling Form

EXERCISE	Exercise 30 minutes each day for 30 days, aim for at least moderate intensity		
Type of Exercise		Duration	_____ minutes
Intensity	☐ Low	☐ Moderate	☐ High

MINDFULNESS	Practice mindfulness at least 10 minutes each day for 30 days
Today's Guided Meditation(s)	

SLEEP	Implement 4 or more of the 6 sleep hygiene practices each day for 30 days		
Implemented These Sleep Hygiene Practices	☐ No electronics 90 min before bed	☐ Sleep mask or blackout shades	☐ Regular bedtime
	☐ No napping	☐ Warm bath/shower prior to bed	☐ Avoid caffeine 10 hrs before bed

SOCIAL CONNECTEDNESS	Meet or call at least two friends or family members each day for 30 days	
	Friends	**Family**
Today's Social Contacts	☐ Call ☐ In-person	☐ Call ☐ In-person

NUTRITION	Log your daily meals/snacks/beverages/ alcohol each day for 30 days	
Logged Meals/Snacks/Beverages/Alcohol	☐ Yes	☐ No
Strongly Recommended		
Implemented MIND Diet Principles	☐ Yes	☐ No
Practiced Mindful Meal Meditation	☐ Breakfast ☐ Lunch ☐ Dinner	

TODAY'S PROGRESS	
My Barrier(s)	
My Solution(s)	

HERO Exercises
Happiness • Enthusiasm • Resilience • Optimism

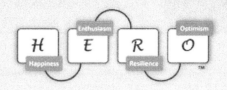

RESILIENCE & OPTIMISM ARE LINKED TO GREATER LIFE SATISFACTION

1. People are quick to point out faults and weaknesses. Acknowledging others' successes is a great way to build and strengthen your resilience while making another person feel great. Think of two people that have recently achieved some type of success, personal or work-related, and write down how you plan to acknowledge their achievement.

   a. _____

   _____

   b. _____

   _____

2. Have you heard of *Paying it Forward*? Someone does something kind for you and you pass it forward by doing something kind for another. Write down two times others have done something kind for you and how that made you feel. Make a plan to pass along those acts of kindness and brighten someone else's day.

   a. _____

   _____

   b. _____

   _____

Please take time to review your previous HERO exercises. Research shows that reflecting on past thoughts about wellness further strengthens and solidifies your HERO wellness traits. The HERO exercises are intentionally repeated every 8 days because repetition is crucial to learning and incorporating new ideas.

Our greatest glory is not in never falling, but in rising every time we fall.
~ Confucius

Daily Journaling Form

EXERCISE	Exercise 30 minutes each day for 30 days, aim for at least moderate intensity		
Type of Exercise		**Duration**	_____ minutes
Intensity	☐ Low	☐ Moderate	☐ High

MINDFULNESS	Practice mindfulness at least 10 minutes each day for 30 days
Today's Guided Meditation(s)	

SLEEP	Implement 4 or more of the 6 sleep hygiene practices each day for 30 days		
Implemented These Sleep Hygiene Practices	☐ No electronics 90 min before bed	☐ Sleep mask or blackout shades	☐ Regular bedtime
	☐ No napping	☐ Warm bath/shower prior to bed	☐ Avoid caffeine 10 hrs before bed

SOCIAL CONNECTEDNESS	Meet or call at least two friends or family members each day for 30 days	
	Friends	**Family**
Today's Social Contacts	☐ Call ☐ In-person	☐ Call ☐ In-person

NUTRITION	Log your daily meals/snacks/beverages/ alcohol each day for 30 days	
Logged Meals/Snacks/Beverages/Alcohol	☐ Yes	☐ No
Strongly Recommended		
Implemented MIND Diet Principles	☐ Yes	☐ No
Practiced Mindful Meal Meditation	☐ Breakfast ☐ Lunch ☐ Dinner	

TODAY'S PROGRESS	
My Barrier(s)	
My Solution(s)	

HERO Exercises
Happiness • Enthusiasm • Resilience • Optimism

HAPPINESS & ENTHUSIASM ARE LINKED TO LONGEVITY

1. To increase your happiness, let's work on strengthening your happiness muscle. Take a moment and write down two positive things that you'd like to experience today. Also, two to three times today, find a few minutes to visualize and relish these positive experiences.

    a. _____

    _____

    b. _____

    _____

2. Having a goal or a project that inspires you will increase your enthusiasm. Write down two projects you find inspiring and set a start date. Put the date on your calendar with reminder alerts – make it happen and watch your enthusiasm improve!

    a. _____

    _____

    b. _____

    _____

Please take time to review your previous HERO exercises. Research shows that reflecting on past thoughts about wellness further strengthens and solidifies your HERO wellness traits. The HERO exercises are intentionally repeated every 8 days because repetition is crucial to learning and incorporating new ideas.

The real secret to success is enthusiasm.
~ Walter Chrysler

Daily Journaling Form

EXERCISE	Exercise 30 minutes each day for 30 days, aim for at least moderate intensity	
Type of Exercise		Duration _____ minutes
Intensity	☐ Low	☐ Moderate ☐ High

MINDFULNESS	Practice mindfulness at least 10 minutes each day for 30 days
Today's Guided Meditation(s)	

SLEEP	Implement 4 or more of the 6 sleep hygiene practices each day for 30 days		
Implemented These Sleep Hygiene Practices	☐ No electronics 90 min before bed	☐ Sleep mask or blackout shades	☐ Regular bedtime
	☐ No napping	☐ Warm bath/shower prior to bed	☐ Avoid caffeine 10 hrs before bed

SOCIAL CONNECTEDNESS	Meet or call at least two friends or family members each day for 30 days			
	Friends		Family	
Today's Social Contacts	☐ Call	☐ In-person	☐ Call	☐ In-person

NUTRITION	Log your daily meals/snacks/beverages/ alcohol each day for 30 days	
Logged Meals/Snacks/Beverages/Alcohol	☐ Yes	☐ No
Strongly Recommended		
Implemented MIND Diet Principles	☐ Yes	☐ No
Practiced Mindful Meal Meditation	☐ Breakfast ☐ Lunch	☐ Dinner

TODAY'S PROGRESS	
My Barrier(s)	
My Solution(s)	

HERO Exercises
Happiness • Enthusiasm • Resilience • Optimism

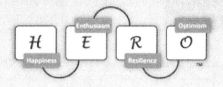

RESILIENT OPTIMISTS HAVE BETTER PHYSICAL HEALTH & BETTER RELATIONSHIPS

1. Resilience means the ability to bounce back from adversities. Write down 2 things about yourself that make you tough, and two skills you have used previously to overcome adversities. Remind yourself throughout the day that you genuinely possess these resilient traits.

   a. _____

   _____

   b. _____

   _____

2. Optimism often requires making a choice about how you view the world. Write down two positive things you want to happen tomorrow, and then spend a few minutes planning on how to make these optimistic attitudes/events a reality.

   a. _____

   _____

   b. _____

   _____

Please take time to review your previous HERO exercises. Research shows that reflecting on past thoughts about wellness further strengthens and solidifies your HERO wellness traits. The HERO exercises are intentionally repeated every 8 days because repetition is crucial to learning and incorporating new ideas.

Happiness is not something readymade. It comes from your own actions.
~ *Dalai Lama*

Phase 1: START - Day 11 - Date: _____

Daily Journaling Form

EXERCISE	Exercise 30 minutes each day for 30 days, aim for at least moderate intensity		
Type of Exercise		Duration	_____ minutes
Intensity	☐ Low	☐ Moderate	☐ High

MINDFULNESS	Practice mindfulness at least 10 minutes each day for 30 days
Today's Guided Meditation(s)	

SLEEP	Implement 4 or more of the 6 sleep hygiene practices each day for 30 days		
Implemented These Sleep Hygiene Practices	☐ No electronics 90 min before bed	☐ Sleep mask or blackout shades	☐ Regular bedtime
	☐ No napping	☐ Warm bath/shower prior to bed	☐ Avoid caffeine 10 hrs before bed

SOCIAL CONNECTEDNESS	Meet or call at least two friends or family members each day for 30 days			
	Friends		**Family**	
Today's Social Contacts	☐ Call	☐ In-person	☐ Call	☐ In-person

NUTRITION	Log your daily meals/snacks/beverages/alcohol each day for 30 days	
Logged Meals/Snacks/Beverages/Alcohol	☐ Yes	☐ No
Strongly Recommended		
Implemented MIND Diet Principles	☐ Yes	☐ No
Practiced Mindful Meal Meditation	☐ Breakfast ☐ Lunch ☐ Dinner	

TODAY'S PROGRESS	
My Barrier(s)	
My Solution(s)	

HERO Exercises
Happiness • Enthusiasm • Resilience • Optimism

HAPPINESS & ENTHUSIASM ARE LINKED TO A STRONGER IMMUNE SYSTEM

1. In today's busy world, it's easy to overlook things that make us happy. Fast-paced lifestyles often become a barrier. Take a moment and mindfully reflect on your day, and write down two things that brought you happiness.

   a. _____

   _____

   b. _____

   _____

2. "Birds of a feather flock together," so surround yourself with happy and enthusiastic people. Write down the names of two people in your life that are happy and enthusiastic. Now, write down how and when you will connect with them.

   a. _____

   _____

   b. _____

   _____

Please take time to review your previous HERO exercises. Research shows that reflecting on past thoughts about wellness further strengthens and solidifies your HERO wellness traits. The HERO exercises are intentionally repeated every 8 days because repetition is crucial to learning and incorporating new ideas.

It is not how much we have, but how much we enjoy, that makes happiness.
~ *Charles Spurgeon*

Daily Journaling Form

EXERCISE	Exercise 30 minutes each day for 30 days, aim for at least moderate intensity		
Type of Exercise		Duration	_____ minutes
Intensity	☐ Low	☐ Moderate	☐ High

MINDFULNESS	Practice mindfulness at least 10 minutes each day for 30 days
Today's Guided Meditation(s)	

SLEEP	Implement 4 or more of the 6 sleep hygiene practices each day for 30 days		
Implemented These Sleep Hygiene Practices	☐ No electronics 90 min before bed	☐ Sleep mask or blackout shades	☐ Regular bedtime
	☐ No napping	☐ Warm bath/shower prior to bed	☐ Avoid caffeine 10 hrs before bed

SOCIAL CONNECTEDNESS	Meet or call at least two friends or family members each day for 30 days			
	Friends		**Family**	
Today's Social Contacts	☐ Call	☐ In-person	☐ Call	☐ In-person

NUTRITION	Log your daily meals/snacks/beverages/ alcohol each day for 30 days	
Logged Meals/Snacks/Beverages/Alcohol	☐ Yes	☐ No
Strongly Recommended		
Implemented MIND Diet Principles	☐ Yes	☐ No
Practiced Mindful Meal Meditation	☐ Breakfast ☐ Lunch	☐ Dinner

TODAY'S PROGRESS	
My Barrier(s)	
My Solution(s)	

HERO Exercises
Happiness • Enthusiasm • Resilience • Optimism

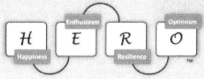

RESILIENT & OPTIMISTIC PEOPLE REPORT BETTER MENTAL HEALTH & LIVE LONGER

1. Dealing with life's challenges with humor builds resilience – the ability to bounce back from life's adversities. Write down two things that happened recently that you found humorous – things that made you smile or laugh.

    a. _____

    _____

    b. _____

    _____

2. Positive affirmations are a great way to build an optimistic mindset. Take a moment and write down two positive statements about yourself, your life, or your future. Purposefully remind yourself of these affirmations several times throughout your day.

    a. _____

    _____

    b. _____

    _____

Please take time to review your previous HERO exercises. Research shows that reflecting on past thoughts about wellness further strengthens and solidifies your HERO wellness traits. The HERO exercises are intentionally repeated every 8 days because repetition is crucial to learning and incorporating new ideas.

Although the world is full of suffering, it is also full of the overcoming of it.
~ Helen Keller

Daily Journaling Form

EXERCISE	Exercise 30 minutes each day for 30 days, aim for at least moderate intensity		
Type of Exercise		Duration	_____ minutes
Intensity	☐ Low	☐ Moderate	☐ High

MINDFULNESS	Practice mindfulness at least 10 minutes each day for 30 days
Today's Guided Meditation(s)	

SLEEP	Implement 4 or more of the 6 sleep hygiene practices each day for 30 days		
Implemented These Sleep Hygiene Practices	☐ No electronics 90 min before bed	☐ Sleep mask or blackout shades	☐ Regular bedtime
	☐ No napping	☐ Warm bath/shower prior to bed	☐ Avoid caffeine 10 hrs before bed

SOCIAL CONNECTEDNESS	Meet or call at least two friends or family members each day for 30 days			
	Friends		**Family**	
Today's Social Contacts	☐	☐	☐	☐
	Call	In-person	Call	In-person

NUTRITION	Log your daily meals/snacks/beverages/ alcohol each day for 30 days	
Logged Meals/Snacks/Beverages/Alcohol	☐ Yes	☐ No
Strongly Recommended		
Implemented MIND Diet Principles	☐ Yes	☐ No
Practiced Mindful Meal Meditation	☐ Breakfast ☐ Lunch	☐ Dinner

TODAY'S PROGRESS	
My Barrier(s)	
My Solution(s)	

HERO Exercises
*H*appiness • *E*nthusiasm • *R*esilience • *O*ptimism

HAPPINESS & ENTHUSIASM ARE KNOWN TO LESSEN PAIN

1. Random acts of kindness will increase your happiness! Take a moment and write down two random acts of kindness you will put into action today. If you don't have time to execute your plan today, be sure to make it happen first thing tomorrow morning.

   a. _____

   _____

   b. _____

   _____

2. When it comes to outlook, do you fall on the positive or the negative side of the fence? Having a positive attitude about life improves enthusiasm. To increase your enthusiasm, mindfully consider your day and write down two examples of your positive attitude and/or actions.

   a. _____

   _____

   b. _____

   _____

Please take time to review your previous HERO exercises. Research shows that reflecting on past thoughts about wellness further strengthens and solidifies your HERO wellness traits. The HERO exercises are intentionally repeated every 8 days because repetition is crucial to learning and incorporating new ideas.

Love is the master key that opens the gates of happiness.
~ *Oliver Wendell Holmes*

Daily Journaling Form

EXERCISE	Exercise 30 minutes each day for 30 days, aim for at least moderate intensity		
Type of Exercise		Duration	_____ minutes
Intensity	☐ Low	☐ Moderate	☐ High

MINDFULNESS	Practice mindfulness at least 10 minutes each day for 30 days
Today's Guided Meditation(s)	

SLEEP	Implement 4 or more of the 6 sleep hygiene practices each day for 30 days		
Implemented These Sleep Hygiene Practices	☐ No electronics 90 min before bed	☐ Sleep mask or blackout shades	☐ Regular bedtime
	☐ No napping	☐ Warm bath/shower prior to bed	☐ Avoid caffeine 10 hrs before bed

SOCIAL CONNECTEDNESS	Meet or call at least two friends or family members each day for 30 days	
	Friends	Family
Today's Social Contacts	☐ Call ☐ In-person	☐ Call ☐ In-person

NUTRITION	Log your daily meals/snacks/beverages/ alcohol each day for 30 days	
Logged Meals/Snacks/Beverages/Alcohol	☐ Yes	☐ No
Strongly Recommended		
Implemented MIND Diet Principles	☐ Yes	☐ No
Practiced Mindful Meal Meditation	☐ Breakfast ☐ Lunch ☐ Dinner	

TODAY'S PROGRESS	
My Barrier(s)	
My Solution(s)	

HERO Exercises
Happiness • Enthusiasm • Resilience • Optimism

H E R O

RESILIENCE & OPTIMISM FERTILIZE A POSITIVE ATTITUDE

1. Being of service to others is a great way to build resilience. List two things you did today (or will do tomorrow) to give back to others or to brighten their day.

   a. _____

   _____

   b. _____

   _____

2. Is your glass half-full or half-empty? How you view the world matters! Write down two things that happened today that you viewed as negative. Take a moment and give this some thought, and then write down a less negative, or even a positive interpretation of the same events.

   a. _____

   _____

   b. _____

   _____

Please take time to review your previous HERO exercises. Research shows that reflecting on past thoughts about wellness further strengthens and solidifies your HERO wellness traits. The HERO exercises are intentionally repeated every 8 days because repetition is crucial to learning and incorporating new ideas.

Man never made any material as resilient as the human spirit.
~ Bern Williams

Daily Journaling Form

EXERCISE	Exercise 30 minutes each day for 30 days, aim for at least moderate intensity	
Type of Exercise		Duration _____ minutes
Intensity	☐ Low ☐ Moderate	☐ High

MINDFULNESS	Practice mindfulness at least 10 minutes each day for 30 days
Today's Guided Meditation(s)	

SLEEP	Implement 4 or more of the 6 sleep hygiene practices each day for 30 days		
Implemented These Sleep Hygiene Practices	☐ No electronics 90 min before bed	☐ Sleep mask or blackout shades	☐ Regular bedtime
	☐ No napping	☐ Warm bath/shower prior to bed	☐ Avoid caffeine 10 hrs before bed

SOCIAL CONNECTEDNESS	Meet or call at least two friends or family members each day for 30 days	
	Friends	Family
Today's Social Contacts	☐ Call ☐ In-person	☐ Call ☐ In-person

NUTRITION	Log your daily meals/snacks/beverages/ alcohol each day for 30 days	
Logged Meals/Snacks/Beverages/Alcohol	☐ Yes	☐ No
Strongly Recommended		
Implemented MIND Diet Principles	☐ Yes	☐ No
Practiced Mindful Meal Meditation	☐ Breakfast ☐ Lunch	☐ Dinner

TODAY'S PROGRESS	
My Barrier(s)	
My Solution(s)	

HERO Exercises
Happiness • Enthusiasm • Resilience • Optimism

HAPPINESS & ENTHUSIASM PREDICT LOWER HEART RATE & BLOOD PRESSURE

1. Thinking about happy memories can positively impact your level of happiness! Write down two memories that bring a smile to your face. Next, spend a few minutes reliving each of these happy memories, and watch your current level of happiness increase.

   a. _____

   _____

   b. _____

   _____

2. Gratitude is known to increase feelings of happiness and enthusiasm. To increase these feelings, mindfully consider your day and write down two examples of things that happened today that increased your feelings of gratitude.

   a. _____

   _____

   b. _____

   _____

Please take time to review your previous HERO exercises. Research shows that reflecting on past thoughts about wellness further strengthens and solidifies your HERO wellness traits. The HERO exercises are intentionally repeated every 8 days because repetition is crucial to learning and incorporating new ideas.

None are so old as those who have outlived enthusiasm.
~ *Henry David Thoreau*

Daily Journaling Form

EXERCISE	Exercise 30 minutes each day for 30 days, aim for at least moderate intensity		
Type of Exercise		Duration	_____ minutes
Intensity	☐ Low	☐ Moderate	☐ High

MINDFULNESS	Practice mindfulness at least 10 minutes each day for 30 days
Today's Guided Meditation(s)	

SLEEP	Implement 4 or more of the 6 sleep hygiene practices each day for 30 days		
Implemented These Sleep Hygiene Practices	☐ No electronics 90 min before bed	☐ Sleep mask or blackout shades	☐ Regular bedtime
	☐ No napping	☐ Warm bath/shower prior to bed	☐ Avoid caffeine 10 hrs before bed

SOCIAL CONNECTEDNESS	Meet or call at least two friends or family members each day for 30 days			
	Friends		Family	
Today's Social Contacts	☐ Call	☐ In-person	☐ Call	☐ In-person

NUTRITION	Log your daily meals/snacks/beverages/ alcohol each day for 30 days	
Logged Meals/Snacks/Beverages/Alcohol	☐ Yes	☐ No
Strongly Recommended		
Implemented MIND Diet Principles	☐ Yes	☐ No
Practiced Mindful Meal Meditation	☐ Breakfast ☐ Lunch	☐ Dinner

TODAY'S PROGRESS	
My Barrier(s)	
My Solution(s)	

HERO Exercises
Happiness • Enthusiasm • Resilience • Optimism

RESILIENCE & OPTIMISM ARE LINKED TO GREATER LIFE SATISFACTION

1. People are quick to point out faults and weaknesses. Acknowledging others' successes is a great way to build and strengthen your resilience while making another person feel great. Think of two people that have recently achieved some type of success, personal or work-related, and write down how you plan to acknowledge their achievement.

   a. _____

   _____

   b. _____

   _____

2. Have you heard of *Paying it Forward*? Someone does something kind for you and you pass it forward by doing something kind for another. Write down two times others have done something kind for you and how that made you feel. Make a plan to pass along those acts of kindness and brighten someone else's day.

   a. _____

   _____

   b. _____

   _____

Please take time to review your previous HERO exercises. Research shows that reflecting on past thoughts about wellness further strengthens and solidifies your HERO wellness traits. The HERO exercises are intentionally repeated every 8 days because repetition is crucial to learning and incorporating new ideas.

Perpetual optimism is a force multiplier.
~ *Colin Powell*

Daily Journaling Form

EXERCISE	Exercise 30 minutes each day for 30 days, aim for at least moderate intensity		
Type of Exercise		Duration	_____ minutes
Intensity	☐ Low	☐ Moderate	☐ High

MINDFULNESS	Practice mindfulness at least 10 minutes each day for 30 days
Today's Guided Meditation(s)	

SLEEP	Implement 4 or more of the 6 sleep hygiene practices each day for 30 days		
Implemented These Sleep Hygiene Practices	☐ No electronics 90 min before bed	☐ Sleep mask or blackout shades	☐ Regular bedtime
	☐ No napping	☐ Warm bath/shower prior to bed	☐ Avoid caffeine 10 hrs before bed

SOCIAL CONNECTEDNESS	Meet or call at least two friends or family members each day for 30 days			
	Friends		Family	
Today's Social Contacts	☐ Call	☐ In-person	☐ Call	☐ In-person

NUTRITION	Log your daily meals/snacks/beverages/ alcohol each day for 30 days	
Logged Meals/Snacks/Beverages/Alcohol	☐ Yes	☐ No
Strongly Recommended		
Implemented MIND Diet Principles	☐ Yes	☐ No
Practiced Mindful Meal Meditation	☐ Breakfast ☐ Lunch ☐ Dinner	

TODAY'S PROGRESS	
My Barrier(s)	
My Solution(s)	

HERO Exercises
Happiness • Enthusiasm • Resilience • Optimism

| HAPPINESS & ENTHUSIASM ARE LINKED TO LONGEVITY |

1. To increase your happiness, let's work on strengthening your happiness muscle. Take a moment and write down two positive things that you'd like to experience today. Also, two to three times today, find a few minutes to visualize and relish these positive experiences.

   a. _____

   _____

   b. _____

   _____

2. Having a goal or a project that inspires you will increase your enthusiasm. Write down two projects you find inspiring and set a start date. Put the date on your calendar with reminder alerts – make it happen and watch your enthusiasm improve!

   a. _____

   _____

   b. _____

   _____

Please take time to review your previous HERO exercises. Research shows that reflecting on past thoughts about wellness further strengthens and solidifies your HERO wellness traits. The HERO exercises are intentionally repeated every 8 days because repetition is crucial to learning and incorporating new ideas.

Enthusiasm is the steam that drives the engine.
~ Napoleon Hill

Daily Journaling Form

EXERCISE	Exercise 30 minutes each day for 30 days, aim for at least moderate intensity		
Type of Exercise		Duration	_____ minutes
Intensity	☐ Low	☐ Moderate	☐ High

MINDFULNESS	Practice mindfulness at least 10 minutes each day for 30 days
Today's Guided Meditation(s)	

SLEEP	Implement 4 or more of the 6 sleep hygiene practices each day for 30 days		
Implemented These Sleep Hygiene Practices	☐ No electronics 90 min before bed	☐ Sleep mask or blackout shades	☐ Regular bedtime
	☐ No napping	☐ Warm bath/shower prior to bed	☐ Avoid caffeine 10 hrs before bed

SOCIAL CONNECTEDNESS	Meet or call at least two friends or family members each day for 30 days			
	Friends		**Family**	
Today's Social Contacts	☐ Call	☐ In-person	☐ Call	☐ In-person

NUTRITION	Log your daily meals/snacks/beverages/alcohol each day for 30 days	
Logged Meals/Snacks/Beverages/Alcohol	☐ Yes	☐ No
Strongly Recommended		
Implemented MIND Diet Principles	☐ Yes	☐ No
Practiced Mindful Meal Meditation	☐ Breakfast ☐ Lunch ☐ Dinner	

TODAY'S PROGRESS	
My Barrier(s)	
My Solution(s)	

HERO Exercises
Happiness • Enthusiasm • Resilience • Optimism

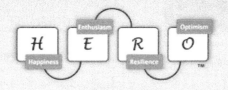

RESILIENT OPTIMISTS HAVE BETTER PHYSICAL HEALTH & BETTER RELATIONSHIPS

---

1. Resilience means the ability to bounce back from adversities. Write down 2 things about yourself that make you tough, and two skills you have used previously to overcome adversities. Remind yourself throughout the day that you genuinely possess these resilient traits.

    a. _____

    _____

    b. _____

    _____

2. Optimism often requires making a choice about how you view the world. Write down two positive things you want to happen tomorrow, and then spend a few minutes planning on how to make these optimistic attitudes/events a reality.

    a. _____

    _____

    b. _____

    _____

Please take time to review your previous HERO exercises. Research shows that reflecting on past thoughts about wellness further strengthens and solidifies your HERO wellness traits. The HERO exercises are intentionally repeated every 8 days because repetition is crucial to learning and incorporating new ideas.

It does not matter how slowly you go so long as you do not stop.
~ Andy Warhol

Daily Journaling Form

EXERCISE	Exercise 30 minutes each day for 30 days, aim for at least moderate intensity		
Type of Exercise		**Duration**	_____ minutes
Intensity	☐ Low	☐ Moderate	☐ High

MINDFULNESS	Practice mindfulness at least 10 minutes each day for 30 days
Today's Guided Meditation(s)	

SLEEP	Implement 4 or more of the 6 sleep hygiene practices each day for 30 days		
Implemented These Sleep Hygiene Practices	☐ No electronics 90 min before bed	☐ Sleep mask or blackout shades	☐ Regular bedtime
	☐ No napping	☐ Warm bath/shower prior to bed	☐ Avoid caffeine 10 hrs before bed

SOCIAL CONNECTEDNESS	Meet or call at least two friends or family members each day for 30 days	
	Friends	**Family**
Today's Social Contacts	☐ Call ☐ In-person	☐ Call ☐ In-person

NUTRITION	Log your daily meals/snacks/beverages/ alcohol each day for 30 days	
Logged Meals/Snacks/Beverages/Alcohol	☐ Yes	☐ No
Strongly Recommended		
Implemented MIND Diet Principles	☐ Yes	☐ No
Practiced Mindful Meal Meditation	☐ Breakfast ☐ Lunch ☐ Dinner	

TODAY'S PROGRESS	
My Barrier(s)	
My Solution(s)	

HERO Exercises
Happiness • Enthusiasm • Resilience • Optimism

| HAPPINESS & ENTHUSIASM ARE LINKED TO A STRONGER IMMUNE SYSTEM |

1. In today's busy world, it's easy to overlook things that make us happy. Fast-paced lifestyles often become a barrier. Take a moment and mindfully reflect on your day, and write down two things that brought you happiness.

    a. _____

    _____

    b. _____

    _____

2. "Birds of a feather flock together," so surround yourself with happy and enthusiastic people. Write down the names of two people in your life that are happy and enthusiastic. Now, write down how and when you will connect with them.

    a. _____

    _____

    b. _____

    _____

Please take time to review your previous HERO exercises. Research shows that reflecting on past thoughts about wellness further strengthens and solidifies your HERO wellness traits. The HERO exercises are intentionally repeated every 8 days because repetition is crucial to learning and incorporating new ideas.

Learn to let go. That is the key to happiness.
~ *Buddha*

Daily Journaling Form

EXERCISE	Exercise 30 minutes each day for 30 days, aim for at least moderate intensity		
Type of Exercise		Duration	_____ minutes
Intensity	☐ Low	☐ Moderate	☐ High

MINDFULNESS	Practice mindfulness at least 10 minutes each day for 30 days
Today's Guided Meditation(s)	

SLEEP	Implement 4 or more of the 6 sleep hygiene practices each day for 30 days		
Implemented These Sleep Hygiene Practices	☐ No electronics 90 min before bed	☐ Sleep mask or blackout shades	☐ Regular bedtime
	☐ No napping	☐ Warm bath/shower prior to bed	☐ Avoid caffeine 10 hrs before bed

SOCIAL CONNECTEDNESS	Meet or call at least two friends or family members each day for 30 days	
	Friends	**Family**
Today's Social Contacts	☐ Call ☐ In-person	☐ Call ☐ In-person

NUTRITION	Log your daily meals/snacks/beverages/ alcohol each day for 30 days	
Logged Meals/Snacks/Beverages/Alcohol	☐ Yes	☐ No
Strongly Recommended		
Implemented MIND Diet Principles	☐ Yes	☐ No
Practiced Mindful Meal Meditation	☐ Breakfast ☐ Lunch ☐ Dinner	

TODAY'S PROGRESS	
My Barrier(s)	
My Solution(s)	

HERO Exercises
Happiness • Enthusiasm • Resilience • Optimism

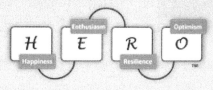

RESILIENT & OPTIMISTIC PEOPLE REPORT BETTER MENTAL HEALTH & LIVE LONGER

1. Dealing with life's challenges with humor builds resilience – the ability to bounce back from life's adversities. Write down two things that happened recently that you found humorous – things that made you smile or laugh.

    a. _____

    _____

    b. _____

    _____

2. Positive affirmations are a great way to build an optimistic mindset. Take a moment and write down two positive statements about yourself, your life, or your future. Purposefully remind yourself of these affirmations several times throughout your day.

    a. _____

    _____

    b. _____

    _____

Please take time to review your previous HERO exercises. Research shows that reflecting on past thoughts about wellness further strengthens and solidifies your HERO wellness traits. The HERO exercises are intentionally repeated every 8 days because repetition is crucial to learning and incorporating new ideas.

Don't leave home without it...YOU were born with Bounce-Back Ability!
~ Ty Howard

Daily Journaling Form

EXERCISE	Exercise 30 minutes each day for 30 days, aim for at least moderate intensity	
Type of Exercise		Duration _____ minutes
Intensity	☐ Low ☐ Moderate	☐ High

MINDFULNESS	Practice mindfulness at least 10 minutes each day for 30 days
Today's Guided Meditation(s)	

SLEEP	Implement 4 or more of the 6 sleep hygiene practices each day for 30 days		
Implemented These Sleep Hygiene Practices	☐ No electronics 90 min before bed	☐ Sleep mask or blackout shades	☐ Regular bedtime
	☐ No napping	☐ Warm bath/shower prior to bed	☐ Avoid caffeine 10 hrs before bed

SOCIAL CONNECTEDNESS	Meet or call at least two friends or family members each day for 30 days			
	Friends		Family	
Today's Social Contacts	☐ Call	☐ In-person	☐ Call	☐ In-person

NUTRITION	Log your daily meals/snacks/beverages/ alcohol each day for 30 days	
Logged Meals/Snacks/Beverages/Alcohol	☐ Yes	☐ No
Strongly Recommended		
Implemented MIND Diet Principles	☐ Yes	☐ No
Practiced Mindful Meal Meditation	☐ Breakfast ☐ Lunch ☐ Dinner	

TODAY'S PROGRESS	
My Barrier(s)	
My Solution(s)	

HERO Exercises
Happiness • Enthusiasm • Resilience • Optimism

HERO

HAPPINESS & ENTHUSIASM ARE KNOWN TO LESSEN PAIN

1. Random acts of kindness will increase your happiness! Take a moment and write down two random acts of kindness you will put into action today. If you don't have time to execute your plan today, be sure to make it happen first thing tomorrow morning.

   a. _____

   _____

   b. _____

   _____

2. When it comes to outlook, do you fall on the positive or the negative side of the fence? Having a positive attitude about life improves enthusiasm. To increase your enthusiasm, mindfully consider your day and write down two examples of your positive attitude and/or actions.

   a. _____

   _____

   b. _____

   _____

Please take time to review your previous HERO exercises. Research shows that reflecting on past thoughts about wellness further strengthens and solidifies your HERO wellness traits. The HERO exercises are intentionally repeated every 8 days because repetition is crucial to learning and incorporating new ideas.

Most smiles are started by another smile.
~ *Frank A. Clark*

Daily Journaling Form

EXERCISE	Exercise 30 minutes each day for 30 days, aim for at least moderate intensity		
Type of Exercise		**Duration**	_____ minutes
Intensity	☐ Low	☐ Moderate	☐ High

MINDFULNESS	Practice mindfulness at least 10 minutes each day for 30 days
Today's Guided Meditation(s)	

SLEEP	Implement 4 or more of the 6 sleep hygiene practices each day for 30 days		
Implemented These Sleep Hygiene Practices	☐ No electronics 90 min before bed	☐ Sleep mask or blackout shades	☐ Regular bedtime
	☐ No napping	☐ Warm bath/shower prior to bed	☐ Avoid caffeine 10 hrs before bed

SOCIAL CONNECTEDNESS	Meet or call at least two friends or family members each day for 30 days			
	Friends		**Family**	
Today's Social Contacts	☐ Call	☐ In-person	☐ Call	☐ In-person

NUTRITION	Log your daily meals/snacks/beverages/ alcohol each day for 30 days	
Logged Meals/Snacks/Beverages/Alcohol	☐ Yes	☐ No
Strongly Recommended		
Implemented MIND Diet Principles	☐ Yes	☐ No
Practiced Mindful Meal Meditation	☐ Breakfast ☐ Lunch ☐ Dinner	

TODAY'S PROGRESS	
My Barrier(s)	
My Solution(s)	

HERO Exercises
Happiness • Enthusiasm • Resilience • Optimism

> ### RESILIENCE & OPTIMISM FERTILIZE A POSITIVE ATTITUDE

1. Being of service to others is a great way to build resilience. List two things you did today (or will do tomorrow) to give back to others or to brighten their day.

   a. _____

   _____

   b. _____

   _____

2. Is your glass half-full or half-empty? How you view the world matters! Write down two things that happened today that you viewed as negative. Take a moment and give this some thought, and then write down a less negative, or even a positive interpretation of the same events.

   a. _____

   _____

   b. _____

   _____

Please take time to review your previous HERO exercises. Research shows that reflecting on past thoughts about wellness further strengthens and solidifies your HERO wellness traits. The HERO exercises are intentionally repeated every 8 days because repetition is crucial to learning and incorporating new ideas.

I have not failed. I've just found 10,000 ways that won't work.
~ *Thomas A. Edison*

Daily Journaling Form

EXERCISE	Exercise 30 minutes each day for 30 days, aim for at least moderate intensity	
Type of Exercise		Duration	_____ minutes
Intensity	☐ Low	☐ Moderate	☐ High

MINDFULNESS	Practice mindfulness at least 10 minutes each day for 30 days
Today's Guided Meditation(s)	

SLEEP	Implement 4 or more of the 6 sleep hygiene practices each day for 30 days		
Implemented These Sleep Hygiene Practices	☐ No electronics 90 min before bed	☐ Sleep mask or blackout shades	☐ Regular bedtime
	☐ No napping	☐ Warm bath/shower prior to bed	☐ Avoid caffeine 10 hrs before bed

SOCIAL CONNECTEDNESS	Meet or call at least two friends or family members each day for 30 days	
	Friends	Family
Today's Social Contacts	☐ Call ☐ In-person	☐ Call ☐ In-person

NUTRITION	Log your daily meals/snacks/beverages/ alcohol each day for 30 days	
Logged Meals/Snacks/Beverages/Alcohol	☐ Yes	☐ No
Strongly Recommended		
Implemented MIND Diet Principles	☐ Yes	☐ No
Practiced Mindful Meal Meditation	☐ Breakfast ☐ Lunch ☐ Dinner	

TODAY'S PROGRESS	
My Barrier(s)	
My Solution(s)	

HERO Exercises
Happiness • Enthusiasm • Resilience • Optimism

H E R O

HAPPINESS & ENTHUSIASM PREDICT LOWER HEART RATE & BLOOD PRESSURE

1. Thinking about happy memories can positively impact your level of happiness! Write down two memories that bring a smile to your face. Next, spend a few minutes reliving each of these happy memories, and watch your current level of happiness increase.

   a. _____

   _____

   b. _____

   _____

2. Gratitude is known to increase feelings of happiness and enthusiasm. To increase these feelings, mindfully consider your day and write down two examples of things that happened today that increased your feelings of gratitude.

   a. _____

   _____

   b. _____

   _____

Please take time to review your previous HERO exercises. Research shows that reflecting on past thoughts about wellness further strengthens and solidifies your HERO wellness traits. The HERO exercises are intentionally repeated every 8 days because repetition is crucial to learning and incorporating new ideas.

I have chosen to be HAPPY because it's good for my HEALTH.
~ Voltaire

Daily Journaling Form

EXERCISE	Exercise 30 minutes each day for 30 days, aim for at least moderate intensity		
Type of Exercise		Duration	_____ minutes
Intensity	☐ Low	☐ Moderate	☐ High

MINDFULNESS	Practice mindfulness at least 10 minutes each day for 30 days
Today's Guided Meditation(s)	

SLEEP	Implement 4 or more of the 6 sleep hygiene practices each day for 30 days		
Implemented These Sleep Hygiene Practices	☐ No electronics 90 min before bed	☐ Sleep mask or blackout shades	☐ Regular bedtime
	☐ No napping	☐ Warm bath/shower prior to bed	☐ Avoid caffeine 10 hrs before bed

SOCIAL CONNECTEDNESS	Meet or call at least two friends or family members each day for 30 days	
	Friends	**Family**
Today's Social Contacts	☐ Call ☐ In-person	☐ Call ☐ In-person

NUTRITION	Log your daily meals/snacks/beverages/alcohol each day for 30 days	
Logged Meals/Snacks/Beverages/Alcohol	☐ Yes	☐ No
Strongly Recommended		
Implemented MIND Diet Principles	☐ Yes	☐ No
Practiced Mindful Meal Meditation	☐ Breakfast ☐ Lunch ☐ Dinner	

TODAY'S PROGRESS	
My Barrier(s)	
My Solution(s)	

HERO Exercises
Happiness • Enthusiasm • Resilience • Optimism

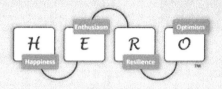

RESILIENCE & OPTIMISM ARE LINKED TO GREATER LIFE SATISFACTION

1. People are quick to point out faults and weaknesses. Acknowledging others' successes is a great way to build and strengthen your resilience while making another person feel great. Think of two people that have recently achieved some type of success, personal or work-related, and write down how you plan to acknowledge their achievement.

   a. _____

   _____

   b. _____

   _____

2. Have you heard of *Paying it Forward*? Someone does something kind for you and you pass it forward by doing something kind for another. Write down two times others have done something kind for you and how that made you feel. Make a plan to pass along those acts of kindness and brighten someone else's day.

   a. _____

   _____

   b. _____

   _____

Please take time to review your previous HERO exercises. Research shows that reflecting on past thoughts about wellness further strengthens and solidifies your HERO wellness traits. The HERO exercises are intentionally repeated every 8 days because repetition is crucial to learning and incorporating new ideas.

Optimism is the best way to see life.
~ *Anonymous*

Daily Journaling Form

EXERCISE	Exercise 30 minutes each day for 30 days, aim for at least moderate intensity		
Type of Exercise		Duration	_____ minutes
Intensity	☐ Low	☐ Moderate	☐ High

MINDFULNESS	Practice mindfulness at least 10 minutes each day for 30 days
Today's Guided Meditation(s)	

SLEEP	Implement 4 or more of the 6 sleep hygiene practices each day for 30 days		
Implemented These Sleep Hygiene Practices	☐ No electronics 90 min before bed	☐ Sleep mask or blackout shades	☐ Regular bedtime
	☐ No napping	☐ Warm bath/shower prior to bed	☐ Avoid caffeine 10 hrs before bed

SOCIAL CONNECTEDNESS	Meet or call at least two friends or family members each day for 30 days			
	Friends		Family	
Today's Social Contacts	☐ Call	☐ In-person	☐ Call	☐ In-person

NUTRITION	Log your daily meals/snacks/beverages/ alcohol each day for 30 days	
Logged Meals/Snacks/Beverages/Alcohol	☐ Yes	☐ No
Strongly Recommended		
Implemented MIND Diet Principles	☐ Yes	☐ No
Practiced Mindful Meal Meditation	☐ Breakfast ☐ Lunch ☐ Dinner	

TODAY'S PROGRESS	
My Barrier(s)	
My Solution(s)	

HERO Exercises
Happiness • Enthusiasm • Resilience • Optimism

HAPPINESS & ENTHUSIASM ARE LINKED TO LONGEVITY

1. To increase your happiness, let's work on strengthening your happiness muscle. Take a moment and write down two positive things that you'd like to experience today. Also, two to three times today, find a few minutes to visualize and relish these positive experiences.

    a. _____

    _____

    b. _____

    _____

2. Having a goal or a project that inspires you will increase your enthusiasm. Write down two projects you find inspiring and set a start date. Put the date on your calendar with reminder alerts – make it happen and watch your enthusiasm improve!

    a. _____

    _____

    b. _____

    _____

Please take time to review your previous HERO exercises. Research shows that reflecting on past thoughts about wellness further strengthens and solidifies your HERO wellness traits. The HERO exercises are intentionally repeated every 8 days because repetition is crucial to learning and incorporating new ideas.

Happiness is the synonym of well-being.
~ Bruce Lee

Daily Journaling Form

EXERCISE	Exercise 30 minutes each day for 30 days, aim for at least moderate intensity	
Type of Exercise	Duration	_____ minutes
Intensity	☐ Low ☐ Moderate ☐ High	

MINDFULNESS	Practice mindfulness at least 10 minutes each day for 30 days
Today's Guided Meditation(s)	

SLEEP	Implement 4 or more of the 6 sleep hygiene practices each day for 30 days				
Implemented These Sleep Hygiene Practices	☐ No electronics 90 min before bed	☐ Sleep mask or blackout shades	☐ Regular bedtime		
	☐ No napping	☐ Warm bath/shower prior to bed	☐ Avoid caffeine 10 hrs before bed		

SOCIAL CONNECTEDNESS	Meet or call at least two friends or family members each day for 30 days			
	Friends		Family	
Today's Social Contacts	☐ Call	☐ In-person	☐ Call	☐ In-person

NUTRITION	Log your daily meals/snacks/beverages/alcohol each day for 30 days	
Logged Meals/Snacks/Beverages/Alcohol	☐ Yes	☐ No
Strongly Recommended		
Implemented MIND Diet Principles	☐ Yes	☐ No
Practiced Mindful Meal Meditation	☐ Breakfast ☐ Lunch ☐ Dinner	

TODAY'S PROGRESS	
My Barrier(s)	
My Solution(s)	

HERO Exercises
*H*appiness • *E*nthusiasm • *R*esilience • *O*ptimism

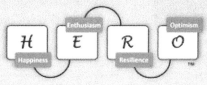

RESILIENT OPTIMISTS HAVE BETTER PHYSICAL HEALTH & BETTER RELATIONSHIPS

1. Resilience means the ability to bounce back from adversities. Write down 2 things about yourself that make you tough, and two skills you have used previously to overcome adversities. Remind yourself throughout the day that you genuinely possess these resilient traits.

   a. _____

   _____

   b. _____

   _____

2. Optimism often requires making a choice about how you view the world. Write down two positive things you want to happen tomorrow, and then spend a few minutes planning on how to make these optimistic attitudes/events a reality.

   a. _____

   _____

   b. _____

   _____

Please take time to review your previous HERO exercises. Research shows that reflecting on past thoughts about wellness further strengthens and solidifies your HERO wellness traits. The HERO exercises are intentionally repeated every 8 days because repetition is crucial to learning and incorporating new ideas.

Optimism is the faith that leads to achievement.
~ *Helen Keller*

Daily Journaling Form

EXERCISE	Exercise 30 minutes each day for 30 days, aim for at least moderate intensity		
Type of Exercise		Duration	_____ minutes
Intensity	☐ Low	☐ Moderate	☐ High

MINDFULNESS	Practice mindfulness at least 10 minutes each day for 30 days
Today's Guided Meditation(s)	

SLEEP	Implement 4 or more of the 6 sleep hygiene practices each day for 30 days		
Implemented These Sleep Hygiene Practices	☐ No electronics 90 min before bed	☐ Sleep mask or blackout shades	☐ Regular bedtime
	☐ No napping	☐ Warm bath/shower prior to bed	☐ Avoid caffeine 10 hrs before bed

SOCIAL CONNECTEDNESS	Meet or call at least two friends or family members each day for 30 days			
	Friends		Family	
Today's Social Contacts	☐ Call	☐ In-person	☐ Call	☐ In-person

NUTRITION	Log your daily meals/snacks/beverages/alcohol each day for 30 days	
Logged Meals/Snacks/Beverages/Alcohol	☐ Yes	☐ No
Strongly Recommended		
Implemented MIND Diet Principles	☐ Yes	☐ No
Practiced Mindful Meal Meditation	☐ Breakfast ☐ Lunch ☐ Dinner	

TODAY'S PROGRESS	
My Barrier(s)	
My Solution(s)	

HERO Exercises
Happiness • Enthusiasm • Resilience • Optimism

HAPPINESS & ENTHUSIASM ARE LINKED TO A STRONGER IMMUNE SYSTEM

1. In today's busy world, it's easy to overlook things that make us happy. Fast-paced lifestyles often become a barrier. Take a moment and mindfully reflect on your day, and write down two things that brought you happiness.

    a. _____

    _____

    b. _____

    _____

2. "Birds of a feather flock together," so surround yourself with happy and enthusiastic people. Write down the names of two people in your life that are happy and enthusiastic. Now, write down how and when you will connect with them.

    a. _____

    _____

    b. _____

    _____

Please take time to review your previous HERO exercises. Research shows that reflecting on past thoughts about wellness further strengthens and solidifies your HERO wellness traits. The HERO exercises are intentionally repeated every 8 days because repetition is crucial to learning and incorporating new ideas.

If you aren't fired with enthusiasm, you'll be fired with enthusiasm.
~ Vincent Lombardi

Daily Journaling Form

EXERCISE	Exercise 30 minutes each day for 30 days, aim for at least moderate intensity		
Type of Exercise		Duration	_____ minutes
Intensity	☐ Low	☐ Moderate	☐ High

MINDFULNESS	Practice mindfulness at least 10 minutes each day for 30 days
Today's Guided Meditation(s)	

SLEEP	Implement 4 or more of the 6 sleep hygiene practices each day for 30 days		
Implemented These Sleep Hygiene Practices	☐ No electronics 90 min before bed	☐ Sleep mask or blackout shades	☐ Regular bedtime
	☐ No napping	☐ Warm bath/shower prior to bed	☐ Avoid caffeine 10 hrs before bed

SOCIAL CONNECTEDNESS	Meet or call at least two friends or family members each day for 30 days	
	Friends	Family
Today's Social Contacts	☐ Call ☐ In-person	☐ Call ☐ In-person

NUTRITION	Log your daily meals/snacks/beverages/ alcohol each day for 30 days	
Logged Meals/Snacks/Beverages/Alcohol	☐ Yes	☐ No
Strongly Recommended		
Implemented MIND Diet Principles	☐ Yes	☐ No
Practiced Mindful Meal Meditation	☐ Breakfast ☐ Lunch ☐ Dinner	

TODAY'S PROGRESS	
My Barrier(s)	
My Solution(s)	

HERO Exercises
Happiness • Enthusiasm • Resilience • Optimism

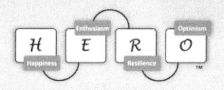

RESILIENT & OPTIMISTIC PEOPLE REPORT BETTER MENTAL HEALTH & LIVE LONGER

1. Dealing with life's challenges with humor builds resilience – the ability to bounce back from life's adversities. Write down two things that happened recently that you found humorous – things that made you smile or laugh.

   a. _____

   _____

   b. _____

   _____

2. Positive affirmations are a great way to build an optimistic mindset. Take a moment and write down two positive statements about yourself, your life, or your future. Purposefully remind yourself of these affirmations several times throughout your day.

   a. _____

   _____

   b. _____

   _____

Please take time to review your previous HERO exercises. Research shows that reflecting on past thoughts about wellness further strengthens and solidifies your HERO wellness traits. The HERO exercises are intentionally repeated every 8 days because repetition is crucial to learning and incorporating new ideas.

Real optimism has reason to complain but prefers to smile.
~ *William Arthur Ward*

Phase 1: START - Day 29 - Date: _____

Daily Journaling Form

EXERCISE	Exercise 30 minutes each day for 30 days, aim for at least moderate intensity		
Type of Exercise		Duration	_____ minutes
Intensity	☐ Low	☐ Moderate	☐ High

MINDFULNESS	Practice mindfulness at least 10 minutes each day for 30 days
Today's Guided Meditation(s)	

SLEEP	Implement 4 or more of the 6 sleep hygiene practices each day for 30 days		
Implemented These Sleep Hygiene Practices	☐ No electronics 90 min before bed	☐ Sleep mask or blackout shades	☐ Regular bedtime
	☐ No napping	☐ Warm bath/shower prior to bed	☐ Avoid caffeine 10 hrs before bed

SOCIAL CONNECTEDNESS	Meet or call at least two friends or family members each day for 30 days			
Today's Social Contacts	Friends ☐ Call	☐ In-person	Family ☐ Call	☐ In-person

NUTRITION	Log your daily meals/snacks/beverages/alcohol each day for 30 days	
Logged Meals/Snacks/Beverages/Alcohol	☐ Yes	☐ No
Strongly Recommended		
Implemented MIND Diet Principles	☐ Yes	☐ No
Practiced Mindful Meal Meditation	☐ Breakfast ☐ Lunch	☐ Dinner

TODAY'S PROGRESS	
My Barrier(s)	
My Solution(s)	

HERO Exercises
Happiness • Enthusiasm • Resilience • Optimism

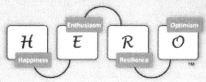

HAPPINESS & ENTHUSIASM ARE KNOWN TO LESSEN PAIN

---

1. Random acts of kindness will increase your happiness! Take a moment and write down two random acts of kindness you will put into action today. If you don't have time to execute your plan today, be sure to make it happen first thing tomorrow morning.

   a. _____

   _____

   b. _____

   _____

---

2. When it comes to outlook, do you fall on the positive or the negative side of the fence? Having a positive attitude about life improves enthusiasm. To increase your enthusiasm, mindfully consider your day and write down two examples of your positive attitude and/or actions.

   a. _____

   _____

   b. _____

   _____

Please take time to review your previous HERO exercises. Research shows that reflecting on past thoughts about wellness further strengthens and solidifies your HERO wellness traits. The HERO exercises are intentionally repeated every 8 days because repetition is crucial to learning and incorporating new ideas.

Happiness is talking to a friend that makes you feel that everything's going to be ok.
~ *Anonymous*

Daily Journaling Form

EXERCISE	Exercise 30 minutes each day for 30 days, aim for at least moderate intensity		
Type of Exercise		Duration	_____ minutes
Intensity	☐ Low	☐ Moderate	☐ High

MINDFULNESS	Practice mindfulness at least 10 minutes each day for 30 days
Today's Guided Meditation(s)	

SLEEP	Implement 4 or more of the 6 sleep hygiene practices each day for 30 days		
Implemented These Sleep Hygiene Practices	☐ No electronics 90 min before bed	☐ Sleep mask or blackout shades	☐ Regular bedtime
	☐ No napping	☐ Warm bath/shower prior to bed	☐ Avoid caffeine 10 hrs before bed

SOCIAL CONNECTEDNESS	Meet or call at least two friends or family members each day for 30 days	
	Friends	Family
Today's Social Contacts	☐ Call ☐ In-person	☐ Call ☐ In-person

NUTRITION	Log your daily meals/snacks/beverages/ alcohol each day for 30 days	
Logged Meals/Snacks/Beverages/Alcohol	☐ Yes	☐ No
Strongly Recommended		
Implemented MIND Diet Principles	☐ Yes	☐ No
Practiced Mindful Meal Meditation	☐ Breakfast ☐ Lunch ☐ Dinner	

TODAY'S PROGRESS	
My Barrier(s)	
My Solution(s)	

HERO Exercises
Happiness • Enthusiasm • Resilience • Optimism

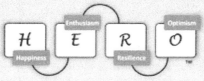

RESILIENCE & OPTIMISM FERTILIZE A POSITIVE ATTITUDE

1. Being of service to others is a great way to build resilience. List two things you did today (or will do tomorrow) to give back to others or to brighten their day.

   a. _____

   _____

   b. _____

   _____

2. Is your glass half-full or half-empty? How you view the world matters! Write down two things that happened today that you viewed as negative. Take a moment and give this some thought, and then write down a less negative, or even a positive interpretation of the same events.

   a. _____

   _____

   b. _____

   _____

Please take time to review your previous HERO exercises. Research shows that reflecting on past thoughts about wellness further strengthens and solidifies your HERO wellness traits. The HERO exercises are intentionally repeated every 8 days because repetition is crucial to learning and incorporating new ideas.

It comes down to perseverance and resiliency.
~ Roger Staubach

HERO Wellness Scale

Day 30

Before you begin Phase 2 of the program, please complete the *HERO Wellness Scale* on the following page. Comparing your Day 1 and Day 30 HERO scores will allow you to measure the progress you've made during the first 30 days of the program.

Please don't underestimate the value of using the *HERO Wellness Scale*, as the feedback will be both useful and motivational.

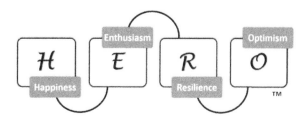

HERO WELLNESS SCALE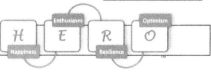

*Please circle **ONE NUMBER** for each question below.*

1. On average, during the last 7 DAYS, how happy have you felt?

0	1	2	3	4	5	6	7	8	9	10

Not at all happy   Mildly happy   Moderately happy   Highly happy   Extremely happy

2. On average, during the last 7 DAYS, how enthusiastic have you felt?

0	1	2	3	4	5	6	7	8	9	10

Not at all enthusiastic   Mildly enthusiastic   Moderately enthusiastic   Highly enthusiastic   Extremely enthusiastic

3. On average, during the last 7 DAYS, how resilient have you felt?

0	1	2	3	4	5	6	7	8	9	10

Not at all resilient   Mildly resilient   Moderately resilient   Highly resilient   Extremely resilient

4. On average, during the last 7 DAYS, how optimistic have you felt?

0	1	2	3	4	5	6	7	8	9	10

Not at all optimistic   Mildly optimistic   Moderately optimistic   Highly optimistic   Extremely optimistic

5. On average, during the last 7 DAYS, how would you rate your mental wellness?

0	1	2	3	4	5	6	7	8	9	10

Not at all good   Mildly good   Moderately good   Markedly good   Extremely good

- -

SCORING: To calculate total score, add all circled numbers.

TOTAL SCORE: 0 - 50

HIGHER SCORES INDICATE HIGHER LEVELS OF WELLNESS

SCORE

WILD 5⭐ Wellness®
Wellness Interventions for Life's Demands

© Copyright 2019 Saundra Jain & Rakesh Jain. All Rights Reserved.

REFLECTIONS on DAY 30

Congratulations! You have successfully completed the first 30 days of LiveWell90. This is a great opportunity to reflect on your first 30 days, allowing you to make minor adjustments regarding any barriers you may have encountered. No matter what your experiences have been during the first 30 days - positive, negative or mixed - we strongly encourage you to take the time to complete this section. We believe you will uncover useful information that may improve the next 30 days of your LiveWell90 experience.

1. What did I learn about myself during the first 30 days of LiveWell90?

_____

_____

_____

_____

_____

2. What sacrifices have I made to meet the program expectations of LiveWell90?

_____

_____

_____

_____

_____

3. What barriers did I encounter?

_____

_____

_____

_____

_____

PLANS for PHASE 2

Now that you have reviewed Phase 1 of your LiveWell90 program, take a moment to answer the questions below. The goal is to identify ways to elevate your LiveWell90 experience.

1. **What can I do to increase the chances that I will successfully complete LiveWell90?**

   _____
   _____
   _____
   _____

2. **To successfully meet the LiveWell90 program expectations, sacrifices are required. Which sacrifice has been the most challenging?**

   _____
   _____
   _____
   _____

3. **List 3-5 ways I can elevate my LiveWell90 experience?**

   _____
   _____
   _____
   _____
   _____
   _____

Words of Advice

*Perfection is **NOT** the goal! Set your goals high and do your best every day. Be kind to yourself as you begin making these changes. Change is never easy. If you miss a day or two, shake it off, regroup, and begin again. Do not throw in the towel. Remember to track your wellness practices using the Participant Tracking Form (page 55).*

Phase 2

SOLIDIFY

- Program Expectations
- Participant Tracking Form
- Daily Journaling & HERO Exercises
- HERO Wellness Scale (Day 60)

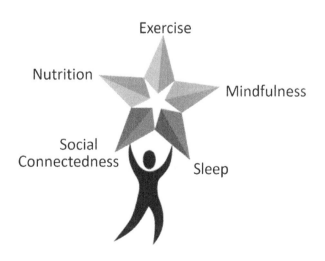

WILD 5☆ Wellness®
Wellness Interventions for Life's Demands

Phase 2
SOLIDIFY

PROGRAM EXPECTATIONS

Exercise	Exercise 30 minutes <u>at least 5 days</u> per week for 30 days, aim for at least moderate intensity*
Mindfulness	Practice mindfulness for at least 10 minutes <u>at least 5 days</u> per week for 30 days
Sleep	Implement 4 or more of the 6 sleep hygiene practices <u>at least 5 days</u> per week for 30 days
Social Connectedness	Meet or call a minimum of two friends or family members <u>at least 5 days</u> per week for 30 days
Nutrition	Log your meals/snacks/beverages/alcohol <u>at least 5 days</u> per week for 30 days [Follow the MIND diet principles as closely as you can]

* *Consult your healthcare provider before starting any exercise program. If you're unable to reach 30 minutes of exercise per day or reach moderate intensity as you begin the program that is fine. Do whatever you're capable of doing. Base the amount of time you exercise and the intensity of your exercise on your physical capabilities.*

WILD 5⭐ Wellness™

Wellness Interventions for Life's Demands

LiveWell90

Participant Tracking Form

Phase 2: SOLIDIFY

Start Date: _____

	Exercise — Did I exercise today following the FID principles?		Mindfulness — Did I mindfully meditate at least 10 minutes today?		Sleep — Did I implement 4 or more of the 6 sleep hygiene practices?		Connectedness — Did I socially connect with at least 2 people today?		Nutrition — Did I log my meals, snacks, and beverages, including alcohol today?		HERO — Did I complete my HERO exercises today?	
	YES	NO	YES	NO	YES	NO	YES	NO	YES	NO	YES	NO
1	○	○	○	○	○	○	○	○	○	○	○	○
2	○	○	○	○	○	○	○	○	○	○	○	○
3	○	○	○	○	○	○	○	○	○	○	○	○
4	○	○	○	○	○	○	○	○	○	○	○	○
5	○	○	○	○	○	○	○	○	○	○	○	○
6	○	○	○	○	○	○	○	○	○	○	○	○
7	○	○	○	○	○	○	○	○	○	○	○	○
8	○	○	○	○	○	○	○	○	○	○	○	○
9	○	○	○	○	○	○	○	○	○	○	○	○
10	○	○	○	○	○	○	○	○	○	○	○	○
11	○	○	○	○	○	○	○	○	○	○	○	○
12	○	○	○	○	○	○	○	○	○	○	○	○
13	○	○	○	○	○	○	○	○	○	○	○	○
14	○	○	○	○	○	○	○	○	○	○	○	○
15	○	○	○	○	○	○	○	○	○	○	○	○
	YES	NO	YES	NO	YES	NO	YES	NO	YES	NO	YES	NO

© Copyright 2019 Saundra Jain & Rakesh Jain. All Rights Reserved.

Day	Exercise		Mindfulness		Sleep		Connectedness		Nutrition		HERO	
	Did I exercise today following the FID principles?		Did I mindfully meditate at least 10 minutes today?		Did I implement 4 or more of the 6 sleep hygiene practices?		Did I socially connect with at least 2 people today?		Did I log my meals, snacks, and beverages, including alcohol today?		Did I complete my HERO exercises today?	
	YES	NO	YES	NO	YES	NO	YES	NO	YES	NO	YES	NO
16	○	○	○	○	○	○	○	○	○	○	○	○
17	○	○	○	○	○	○	○	○	○	○	○	○
18	○	○	○	○	○	○	○	○	○	○	○	○
19	○	○	○	○	○	○	○	○	○	○	○	○
20	○	○	○	○	○	○	○	○	○	○	○	○
21	○	○	○	○	○	○	○	○	○	○	○	○
22	○	○	○	○	○	○	○	○	○	○	○	○
23	○	○	○	○	○	○	○	○	○	○	○	○
24	○	○	○	○	○	○	○	○	○	○	○	○
25	○	○	○	○	○	○	○	○	○	○	○	○
26	○	○	○	○	○	○	○	○	○	○	○	○
27	○	○	○	○	○	○	○	○	○	○	○	○
28	○	○	○	○	○	○	○	○	○	○	○	○
29	○	○	○	○	○	○	○	○	○	○	○	○
30	○	○	○	○	○	○	○	○	○	○	○	○
	YES	NO	YES	NO	YES	NO	YES	NO	YES	NO	YES	NO

© Copyright 2019 Saundra Jain & Rakesh Jain. All Rights Reserved.

132

Daily Journaling and HERO Exercises

Using the *Daily Journaling Form* allows you to capture useful information on a daily basis about your LiveWell90 wellness practices. It asks you to document what you did each day to meet the program expectations for each of the 5 wellness components. You are also asked to record any barriers you encountered, and the solutions you used to overcome them.

HERO exercises are designed to improve your mental wellness. Doing them daily increases and enriches your levels of happiness, enthusiasm, resilience, and optimism.

Daily Journaling Form

EXERCISE	Exercise 30 minutes at least 5 days per week for 30 days, aim for at least moderate intensity

Type of Exercise		Duration	_____ minutes
Intensity	☐ Low	☐ Moderate	☐ High

MINDFULNESS	Practice mindfulness at least 10 minutes at least 5 days per week for 30 days
Today's Guided Meditation(s)	

SLEEP	Implement 4 or more of the 6 sleep hygiene practices at least 5 days per week for 30 days

Implemented These Sleep Hygiene Practices	☐ No electronics 90 min before bed	☐ Sleep mask or blackout shades	☐ Regular bedtime
	☐ No napping	☐ Warm bath/shower prior to bed	☐ Avoid caffeine 10 hrs before bed

SOCIAL CONNECTEDNESS	Meet or call at least two friends or family members at least 5 days per week for 30 days

Today's Social Contacts	Friends		Family	
	☐ Call	☐ In-person	☐ Call	☐ In-person

NUTRITION	Log your daily meals/snacks/beverages/alcohol at least 5 days per week for 30 days

Logged Meals/Snacks/Beverages/Alcohol	☐ Yes	☐ No
Strongly Recommended		
Implemented MIND Diet Principles	☐ Yes	☐ No
Practiced Mindful Meal Meditation	☐ Breakfast ☐ Lunch ☐ Dinner	

TODAY'S PROGRESS	
My Barrier(s)	
My Solution(s)	

HERO Exercises
Happiness • Enthusiasm • Resilience • Optimism

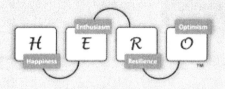

HAPPINESS & ENTHUSIASM PREDICT LOWER HEART RATE & BLOOD PRESSURE

---

1. Thinking about happy memories can positively impact your level of happiness! Write down two memories that bring a smile to your face. Next, spend a few minutes reliving each of these happy memories, and watch your current level of happiness increase.

    a. _____

    _____

    b. _____

    _____

---

2. Gratitude is known to increase feelings of happiness and enthusiasm. To increase these feelings, mindfully consider your day and write down two examples of things that happened today that increased your feelings of gratitude.

    a. _____

    _____

    b. _____

    _____

Please take time to review your previous HERO exercises. Research shows that reflecting on past thoughts about wellness further strengthens and solidifies your HERO wellness traits. The HERO exercises are intentionally repeated every 8 days because repetition is crucial to learning and incorporating new ideas.

An enthusiastic heart finds opportunities everywhere.
~ Paulo Coelho

Daily Journaling Form

EXERCISE	Exercise 30 minutes at least 5 days per week for 30 days, aim for at least moderate intensity		
Type of Exercise		Duration	_____ minutes
Intensity	☐ Low	☐ Moderate	☐ High

MINDFULNESS	Practice mindfulness at least 10 minutes at least 5 days per week for 30 days
Today's Guided Meditation(s)	

SLEEP	Implement 4 or more of the 6 sleep hygiene practices at least 5 days per week for 30 days		
Implemented These Sleep Hygiene Practices	☐ No electronics 90 min before bed	☐ Sleep mask or blackout shades	☐ Regular bedtime
	☐ No napping	☐ Warm bath/shower prior to bed	☐ Avoid caffeine 10 hrs before bed

SOCIAL CONNECTEDNESS	Meet or call at least two friends or family members at least 5 days per week for 30 days	
	Friends	Family
Today's Social Contacts	☐ Call ☐ In-person	☐ Call ☐ In-person

NUTRITION	Log your daily meals/snacks/beverages/alcohol at least 5 days per week for 30 days	
Logged Meals/Snacks/Beverages/Alcohol	☐ Yes	☐ No
Strongly Recommended		
Implemented MIND Diet Principles	☐ Yes	☐ No
Practiced Mindful Meal Meditation	☐ Breakfast ☐ Lunch ☐ Dinner	

TODAY'S PROGRESS	
My Barrier(s)	
My Solution(s)	

HERO Exercises
Happiness • Enthusiasm • Resilience • Optimism

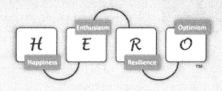

RESILIENT OPTIMISTS HAVE BETTER PHYSICAL HEALTH & BETTER RELATIONSHIPS

1. Resilience means the ability to bounce back from adversities. Write down 2 things about yourself that make you tough, and two skills you have used previously to overcome adversities. Remind yourself throughout the day that you genuinely possess these resilient traits.

   a. _____

   _____

   b. _____

   _____

2. Optimism often requires making a choice about how you view the world. Write down two positive things you want to happen tomorrow, and then spend a few minutes planning on how to make these optimistic attitudes/events a reality.

   a. _____

   _____

   b. _____

   _____

Please take time to review your previous HERO exercises. Research shows that reflecting on past thoughts about wellness further strengthens and solidifies your HERO wellness traits. The HERO exercises are intentionally repeated every 8 days because repetition is crucial to learning and incorporating new ideas.

Choose to be optimistic, it feels better.
~ Dalai Lama XIV

Daily Journaling Form

EXERCISE	Exercise 30 minutes at least 5 days per week for 30 days, aim for at least moderate intensity

Type of Exercise		Duration	_____ minutes
Intensity	☐ Low	☐ Moderate	☐ High

MINDFULNESS	Practice mindfulness at least 10 minutes at least 5 days per week for 30 days

Today's Guided Meditation(s)	

SLEEP	Implement 4 or more of the 6 sleep hygiene practices at least 5 days per week for 30 days

Implemented These Sleep Hygiene Practices	☐ No electronics 90 min before bed	☐ Sleep mask or blackout shades	☐ Regular bedtime
	☐ No napping	☐ Warm bath/shower prior to bed	☐ Avoid caffeine 10 hrs before bed

SOCIAL CONNECTEDNESS	Meet or call at least two friends or family members at least 5 days per week for 30 days

	Friends		Family	
Today's Social Contacts	☐ Call	☐ In-person	☐ Call	☐ In-person

NUTRITION	Log your daily meals/snacks/beverages/ alcohol at least 5 days per week for 30 days

Logged Meals/Snacks/Beverages/Alcohol	☐ Yes	☐ No
Strongly Recommended		
Implemented MIND Diet Principles	☐ Yes	☐ No
Practiced Mindful Meal Meditation	☐ Breakfast ☐ Lunch ☐ Dinner	

TODAY'S PROGRESS	
My Barrier(s)	
My Solution(s)	

HERO Exercises
Happiness • Enthusiasm • Resilience • Optimism

HAPPINESS & ENTHUSIASM ARE LINKED TO LONGEVITY

1. To increase your happiness, let's work on strengthening your happiness muscle. Take a moment and write down two positive things that you'd like to experience today. Also, two to three times today, find a few minutes to visualize and relish these positive experiences.

    a. _____

       _____

    b. _____

       _____

2. Having a goal or a project that inspires you will increase your enthusiasm. Write down two projects you find inspiring and set a start date. Put the date on your calendar with reminder alerts – make it happen and watch your enthusiasm improve!

    a. _____

       _____

    b. _____

       _____

Please take time to review your previous HERO exercises. Research shows that reflecting on past thoughts about wellness further strengthens and solidifies your HERO wellness traits. The HERO exercises are intentionally repeated every 8 days because repetition is crucial to learning and incorporating new ideas.

Happiness is the secret to all beauty. There is no beauty without happiness.
~ *Christian Dior*

Daily Journaling Form

EXERCISE	Exercise 30 minutes at least 5 days per week for 30 days, aim for at least moderate intensity		
Type of Exercise		Duration	_____ minutes
Intensity	☐ Low	☐ Moderate	☐ High

MINDFULNESS	Practice mindfulness at least 10 minutes at least 5 days per week for 30 days
Today's Guided Meditation(s)	

SLEEP	Implement 4 or more of the 6 sleep hygiene practices at least 5 days per week for 30 days				
Implemented These Sleep Hygiene Practices	☐ No electronics 90 min before bed	☐ Sleep mask or blackout shades	☐ Regular bedtime		
	☐ No napping	☐ Warm bath/shower prior to bed	☐ Avoid caffeine 10 hrs before bed		

SOCIAL CONNECTEDNESS	Meet or call at least two friends or family members at least 5 days per week for 30 days			
Today's Social Contacts	**Friends**		**Family**	
	☐ Call	☐ In-person	☐ Call	☐ In-person

NUTRITION	Log your daily meals/snacks/beverages/ alcohol at least 5 days per week for 30 days		
Logged Meals/Snacks/Beverages/Alcohol	☐ Yes		☐ No
Strongly Recommended			
Implemented MIND Diet Principles	☐ Yes		☐ No
Practiced Mindful Meal Meditation	☐ Breakfast	☐ Lunch	☐ Dinner

TODAY'S PROGRESS	
My Barrier(s)	
My Solution(s)	

HERO Exercises
*H*appiness • *E*nthusiasm • *R*esilience • *O*ptimism

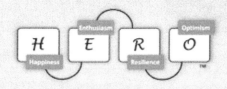

RESILIENT OPTIMISTS HAVE BETTER PHYSICAL HEALTH & BETTER RELATIONSHIPS

1. Resilience means the ability to bounce back from adversities. Write down 2 things about yourself that make you tough, and two skills you have used previously to overcome adversities. Remind yourself throughout the day that you genuinely possess these resilient traits.

   a. _____

   _____

   b. _____

   _____

2. Optimism often requires making a choice about how you view the world. Write down two positive things you want to happen tomorrow, and then spend a few minutes planning on how to make these optimistic attitudes/events a reality.

   a. _____

   _____

   b. _____

   _____

Please take time to review your previous HERO exercises. Research shows that reflecting on past thoughts about wellness further strengthens and solidifies your HERO wellness traits. The HERO exercises are intentionally repeated every 8 days because repetition is crucial to learning and incorporating new ideas.

I was reminded that my blood type is Be Positive.
~ *Anonymous*

Daily Journaling Form

EXERCISE	Exercise 30 minutes at least 5 days per week for 30 days, aim for at least moderate intensity

Type of Exercise		Duration	_____ minutes
Intensity	☐ Low	☐ Moderate	☐ High

MINDFULNESS	Practice mindfulness at least 10 minutes at least 5 days per week for 30 days

Today's Guided Meditation(s)	

SLEEP	Implement 4 or more of the 6 sleep hygiene practices at least 5 days per week for 30 days

Implemented These Sleep Hygiene Practices	☐ No electronics 90 min before bed	☐ Sleep mask or blackout shades	☐ Regular bedtime
	☐ No napping	☐ Warm bath/shower prior to bed	☐ Avoid caffeine 10 hrs before bed

SOCIAL CONNECTEDNESS	Meet or call at least two friends or family members at least 5 days per week for 30 days

Today's Social Contacts	Friends		Family	
	☐ Call	☐ In-person	☐ Call	☐ In-person

NUTRITION	Log your daily meals/snacks/beverages/alcohol at least 5 days per week for 30 days

Logged Meals/Snacks/Beverages/Alcohol	☐ Yes	☐ No
Strongly Recommended		
Implemented MIND Diet Principles	☐ Yes	☐ No
Practiced Mindful Meal Meditation	☐ Breakfast ☐ Lunch ☐ Dinner	

TODAY'S PROGRESS	
My Barrier(s)	
My Solution(s)	

HERO Exercises
Happiness • Enthusiasm • Resilience • Optimism

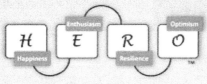

HAPPINESS & ENTHUSIASM ARE LINKED TO A STRONGER IMMUNE SYSTEM

1. In today's busy world, it's easy to overlook things that make us happy. Fast-paced lifestyles often become a barrier. Take a moment and mindfully reflect on your day, and write down two things that brought you happiness.

   a. _____

   _____

   b. _____

   _____

2. "Birds of a feather flock together," so surround yourself with happy and enthusiastic people. Write down the names of two people in your life that are happy and enthusiastic. Now, write down how and when you will connect with them.

   a. _____

   _____

   b. _____

   _____

Please take time to review your previous HERO exercises. Research shows that reflecting on past thoughts about wellness further strengthens and solidifies your HERO wellness traits. The HERO exercises are intentionally repeated every 8 days because repetition is crucial to learning and incorporating new ideas.

To love and to be loved is the greatest happiness of existence.
~ *Sydney Smith*

Daily Journaling Form

EXERCISE	Exercise 30 minutes <u>at least 5 days</u> per week for 30 days, aim for at least moderate intensity

Type of Exercise		Duration	_____ minutes
Intensity	☐ Low	☐ Moderate	☐ High

MINDFULNESS	Practice mindfulness at least 10 minutes <u>at least 5 days</u> per week for 30 days

Today's Guided Meditation(s)	

SLEEP	Implement 4 or more of the 6 sleep hygiene practices <u>at least 5 days</u> per week for 30 days

Implemented These Sleep Hygiene Practices	☐ No electronics 90 min before bed	☐ Sleep mask or blackout shades	☐ Regular bedtime
	☐ No napping	☐ Warm bath/shower prior to bed	☐ Avoid caffeine 10 hrs before bed

SOCIAL CONNECTEDNESS	Meet or call at least two friends or family members <u>at least 5 days</u> per week for 30 days

Today's Social Contacts	Friends		Family	
	☐ Call	☐ In-person	☐ Call	☐ In-person

NUTRITION	Log your daily meals/snacks/beverages/alcohol <u>at least 5 days</u> per week for 30 days

Logged Meals/Snacks/Beverages/Alcohol	☐ Yes	☐ No
Strongly Recommended		
Implemented MIND Diet Principles	☐ Yes	☐ No
Practiced Mindful Meal Meditation	☐ Breakfast ☐ Lunch ☐ Dinner	

TODAY'S PROGRESS	
My Barrier(s)	
My Solution(s)	

HERO Exercises
Happiness • Enthusiasm • Resilience • Optimism

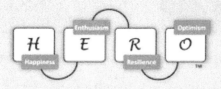

RESILIENT & OPTIMISTIC PEOPLE REPORT BETTER MENTAL HEALTH & LIVE LONGER

1. Dealing with life's challenges with humor builds resilience – the ability to bounce back from life's adversities. Write down two things that happened recently that you found humorous – things that made you smile or laugh.

   a. _____

   _____

   b. _____

   _____

2. Positive affirmations are a great way to build an optimistic mindset. Take a moment and write down two positive statements about yourself, your life, or your future. Purposefully remind yourself of these affirmations several times throughout your day.

   a. _____

   _____

   b. _____

   _____

Please take time to review your previous HERO exercises. Research shows that reflecting on past thoughts about wellness further strengthens and solidifies your HERO wellness traits. The HERO exercises are intentionally repeated every 8 days because repetition is crucial to learning and incorporating new ideas.

An optimist is someone who expects all the crayons to be in the box.
~ *Emily Strawn*

Daily Journaling Form

EXERCISE	Exercise 30 minutes at least 5 days per week for 30 days, aim for at least moderate intensity		
Type of Exercise		Duration	_____ minutes
Intensity	☐ Low	☐ Moderate	☐ High

MINDFULNESS	Practice mindfulness at least 10 minutes at least 5 days per week for 30 days
Today's Guided Meditation(s)	

SLEEP	Implement 4 or more of the 6 sleep hygiene practices at least 5 days per week for 30 days		
Implemented These Sleep Hygiene Practices	☐ No electronics 90 min before bed	☐ Sleep mask or blackout shades	☐ Regular bedtime
	☐ No napping	☐ Warm bath/shower prior to bed	☐ Avoid caffeine 10 hrs before bed

SOCIAL CONNECTEDNESS	Meet or call at least two friends or family members at least 5 days per week for 30 days			
	Friends		Family	
Today's Social Contacts	☐ Call	☐ In-person	☐ Call	☐ In-person

NUTRITION	Log your daily meals/snacks/beverages/alcohol at least 5 days per week for 30 days	
Logged Meals/Snacks/Beverages/Alcohol	☐ Yes	☐ No
Strongly Recommended		
Implemented MIND Diet Principles	☐ Yes	☐ No
Practiced Mindful Meal Meditation	☐ Breakfast ☐ Lunch ☐ Dinner	

TODAY'S PROGRESS	
My Barrier(s)	
My Solution(s)	

HERO Exercises
Happiness • Enthusiasm • Resilience • Optimism

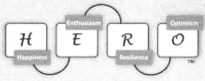

HAPPINESS & ENTHUSIASM ARE KNOWN TO LESSEN PAIN

1. Random acts of kindness will increase your happiness! Take a moment and write down two random acts of kindness you will put into action today. If you don't have time to execute your plan today, be sure to make it happen first thing tomorrow morning.

   a. _____

   _____

   b. _____

   _____

2. When it comes to outlook, do you fall on the positive or the negative side of the fence? Having a positive attitude about life improves enthusiasm. To increase your enthusiasm, mindfully consider your day and write down two examples of your positive attitude and/or actions.

   a. _____

   _____

   b. _____

   _____

Please take time to review your previous HERO exercises. Research shows that reflecting on past thoughts about wellness further strengthens and solidifies your HERO wellness traits. The HERO exercises are intentionally repeated every 8 days because repetition is crucial to learning and incorporating new ideas.

Enthusiasm is the yeast that makes your hopes rise to the stars.
~ *Henry Ford*

Daily Journaling Form

EXERCISE	Exercise 30 minutes <u>at least 5 days</u> per week for 30 days, aim for at least moderate intensity		
Type of Exercise		Duration	_____ minutes
Intensity	☐ Low	☐ Moderate	☐ High

MINDFULNESS	Practice mindfulness at least 10 minutes <u>at least 5 days</u> per week for 30 days
Today's Guided Meditation(s)	

SLEEP	Implement 4 or more of the 6 sleep hygiene practices <u>at least 5 days</u> per week for 30 days		
Implemented These Sleep Hygiene Practices	☐ No electronics 90 min before bed	☐ Sleep mask or blackout shades	☐ Regular bedtime
	☐ No napping	☐ Warm bath/shower prior to bed	☐ Avoid caffeine 10 hrs before bed

SOCIAL CONNECTEDNESS	Meet or call at least two friends or family members <u>at least 5 days</u> per week for 30 days	
Today's Social Contacts	**Friends** ☐ Call ☐ In-person	**Family** ☐ Call ☐ In-person

NUTRITION	Log your daily meals/snacks/beverages/ alcohol <u>at least 5 days</u> per week for 30 days	
Logged Meals/Snacks/Beverages/Alcohol	☐ Yes	☐ No
Strongly Recommended		
Implemented MIND Diet Principles	☐ Yes	☐ No
Practiced Mindful Meal Meditation	☐ Breakfast ☐ Lunch ☐ Dinner	

TODAY'S PROGRESS	
My Barrier(s)	
My Solution(s)	

HERO Exercises
Happiness • Enthusiasm • Resilience • Optimism

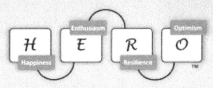

RESILIENCE & OPTIMISM FERTILIZE A POSITIVE ATTITUDE

1. Being of service to others is a great way to build resilience. List two things you did today (or will do tomorrow) to give back to others or to brighten their day.

    a. _____

       _____

    b. _____

       _____

2. Is your glass half-full or half-empty? How you view the world matters! Write down two things that happened today that you viewed as negative. Take a moment and give this some thought, and then write down a less negative, or even a positive interpretation of the same events.

    a. _____

       _____

    b. _____

       _____

Please take time to review your previous HERO exercises. Research shows that reflecting on past thoughts about wellness further strengthens and solidifies your HERO wellness traits. The HERO exercises are intentionally repeated every 8 days because repetition is crucial to learning and incorporating new ideas.

The optimist sees the donut; the pessimist sees the hole.
~ *Oscar Wilde*

Daily Journaling Form

EXERCISE	Exercise 30 minutes at least 5 days per week for 30 days, aim for at least moderate intensity		
Type of Exercise		Duration	_____ minutes
Intensity	☐ Low	☐ Moderate	☐ High

MINDFULNESS	Practice mindfulness at least 10 minutes at least 5 days per week for 30 days
Today's Guided Meditation(s)	

SLEEP	Implement 4 or more of the 6 sleep hygiene practices at least 5 days per week for 30 days		
Implemented These Sleep Hygiene Practices	☐ No electronics 90 min before bed	☐ Sleep mask or blackout shades	☐ Regular bedtime
	☐ No napping	☐ Warm bath/shower prior to bed	☐ Avoid caffeine 10 hrs before bed

SOCIAL CONNECTEDNESS	Meet or call at least two friends or family members at least 5 days per week for 30 days	
	Friends	**Family**
Today's Social Contacts	☐ Call ☐ In-person	☐ Call ☐ In-person

NUTRITION	Log your daily meals/snacks/beverages/ alcohol at least 5 days per week for 30 days	
Logged Meals/Snacks/Beverages/Alcohol	☐ Yes	☐ No
Strongly Recommended		
Implemented MIND Diet Principles	☐ Yes	☐ No
Practiced Mindful Meal Meditation	☐ Breakfast ☐ Lunch ☐ Dinner	

TODAY'S PROGRESS	
My Barrier(s)	
My Solution(s)	

HERO Exercises
Happiness • Enthusiasm • Resilience • Optimism

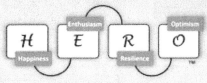

HAPPINESS & ENTHUSIASM PREDICT LOWER HEART RATE & BLOOD PRESSURE

---

1. Thinking about happy memories can positively impact your level of happiness! Write down two memories that bring a smile to your face. Next, spend a few minutes reliving each of these happy memories, and watch your current level of happiness increase.

    a. _____

    _____

    b. _____

    _____

---

2. Gratitude is known to increase feelings of happiness and enthusiasm. To increase these feelings, mindfully consider your day and write down two examples of things that happened today that increased your feelings of gratitude.

    a. _____

    _____

    b. _____

    _____

Please take time to review your previous HERO exercises. Research shows that reflecting on past thoughts about wellness further strengthens and solidifies your HERO wellness traits. The HERO exercises are intentionally repeated every 8 days because repetition is crucial to learning and incorporating new ideas.

Man never rises to great truths without enthusiasm.
~ Marquis de Vauvenargues

Daily Journaling Form

EXERCISE	Exercise 30 minutes <u>at least 5 days</u> per week for 30 days, aim for at least moderate intensity
Type of Exercise		Duration	_____ minutes
Intensity	☐ Low ☐ Moderate ☐ High

MINDFULNESS	Practice mindfulness at least 10 minutes <u>at least 5 days</u> per week for 30 days
Today's Guided Meditation(s)	

SLEEP	Implement 4 or more of the 6 sleep hygiene practices <u>at least 5 days</u> per week for 30 days
Implemented These Sleep Hygiene Practices	☐ No electronics 90 min before bed ☐ Sleep mask or blackout shades ☐ Regular bedtime ☐ No napping ☐ Warm bath/shower prior to bed ☐ Avoid caffeine 10 hrs before bed

SOCIAL CONNECTEDNESS — Meet or call at least two friends or family members <u>at least 5 days</u> per week for 30 days

	Friends		Family	
Today's Social Contacts	☐ Call	☐ In-person	☐ Call	☐ In-person

NUTRITION	Log your daily meals/snacks/beverages/ alcohol <u>at least 5 days</u> per week for 30 days
Logged Meals/Snacks/Beverages/Alcohol	☐ Yes ☐ No
Strongly Recommended	
Implemented MIND Diet Principles	☐ Yes ☐ No
Practiced Mindful Meal Meditation	☐ Breakfast ☐ Lunch ☐ Dinner

TODAY'S PROGRESS	
My Barrier(s)	
My Solution(s)	

HERO Exercises
Happiness • Enthusiasm • Resilience • Optimism

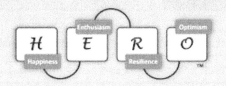

RESILIENCE & OPTIMISM ARE LINKED TO GREATER LIFE SATISFACTION

---

1. People are quick to point out faults and weaknesses. Acknowledging others' successes is a great way to build and strengthen your resilience while making another person feel great. Think of two people that have recently achieved some type of success, personal or work-related, and write down how you plan to acknowledge their achievement.

   a. _____

   _____

   b. _____

   _____

---

2. Have you heard of *Paying it Forward*? Someone does something kind for you and you pass it forward by doing something kind for another. Write down two times others have done something kind for you and how that made you feel. Make a plan to pass along those acts of kindness and brighten someone else's day.

   a. _____

   _____

   b. _____

   _____

Please take time to review your previous HERO exercises. Research shows that reflecting on past thoughts about wellness further strengthens and solidifies your HERO wellness traits. The HERO exercises are intentionally repeated every 8 days because repetition is crucial to learning and incorporating new ideas.

When you choose to connect with others under stress, you can create resilience.
~ Kelly McGonigal

Daily Journaling Form

EXERCISE	Exercise 30 minutes <u>at least 5 days</u> per week for 30 days, aim for at least moderate intensity		
Type of Exercise		**Duration**	_____ minutes
Intensity	☐ Low	☐ Moderate	☐ High

MINDFULNESS	Practice mindfulness at least 10 minutes <u>at least 5 days</u> per week for 30 days
Today's Guided Meditation(s)	

SLEEP	Implement 4 or more of the 6 sleep hygiene practices <u>at least 5 days</u> per week for 30 days		
Implemented These Sleep Hygiene Practices	☐ No electronics 90 min before bed	☐ Sleep mask or blackout shades	☐ Regular bedtime
	☐ No napping	☐ Warm bath/shower prior to bed	☐ Avoid caffeine 10 hrs before bed

SOCIAL CONNECTEDNESS	Meet or call at least two friends or family members <u>at least 5 days</u> per week for 30 days	
	Friends	**Family**
Today's Social Contacts	☐ Call ☐ In-person	☐ Call ☐ In-person

NUTRITION	Log your daily meals/snacks/beverages/ alcohol <u>at least 5 days</u> per week for 30 days	
Logged Meals/Snacks/Beverages/Alcohol	☐ Yes	☐ No
Strongly Recommended		
Implemented MIND Diet Principles	☐ Yes	☐ No
Practiced Mindful Meal Meditation	☐ Breakfast ☐ Lunch ☐ Dinner	

TODAY'S PROGRESS	
My Barrier(s)	
My Solution(s)	

HERO Exercises
Happiness • Enthusiasm • Resilience • Optimism

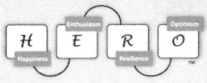

HAPPINESS & ENTHUSIASM ARE LINKED TO LONGEVITY

1. To increase your happiness, let's work on strengthening your happiness muscle. Take a moment and write down two positive things that you'd like to experience today. Also, two to three times today, find a few minutes to visualize and relish these positive experiences.

   a. _____

   _____

   b. _____

   _____

2. Having a goal or a project that inspires you will increase your enthusiasm. Write down two projects you find inspiring and set a start date. Put the date on your calendar with reminder alerts – make it happen and watch your enthusiasm improve!

   a. _____

   _____

   b. _____

   _____

Please take time to review your previous HERO exercises. Research shows that reflecting on past thoughts about wellness further strengthens and solidifies your HERO wellness traits. The HERO exercises are intentionally repeated every 8 days because repetition is crucial to learning and incorporating new ideas.

I choose to be happy today.
~ Anonymous

Daily Journaling Form

EXERCISE	Exercise 30 minutes at least 5 days per week for 30 days, aim for at least moderate intensity		
Type of Exercise		Duration	_____ minutes
Intensity	☐ Low	☐ Moderate	☐ High

MINDFULNESS	Practice mindfulness at least 10 minutes at least 5 days per week for 30 days
Today's Guided Meditation(s)	

SLEEP	Implement 4 or more of the 6 sleep hygiene practices at least 5 days per week for 30 days		
Implemented These Sleep Hygiene Practices	☐ No electronics 90 min before bed	☐ Sleep mask or blackout shades	☐ Regular bedtime
	☐ No napping	☐ Warm bath/shower prior to bed	☐ Avoid caffeine 10 hrs before bed

SOCIAL CONNECTEDNESS	Meet or call at least two friends or family members at least 5 days per week for 30 days	
	Friends	Family
Today's Social Contacts	☐ Call ☐ In-person	☐ Call ☐ In-person

NUTRITION	Log your daily meals/snacks/beverages/alcohol at least 5 days per week for 30 days	
Logged Meals/Snacks/Beverages/Alcohol	☐ Yes	☐ No
Strongly Recommended		
Implemented MIND Diet Principles	☐ Yes	☐ No
Practiced Mindful Meal Meditation	☐ Breakfast ☐ Lunch ☐ Dinner	

TODAY'S PROGRESS	
My Barrier(s)	
My Solution(s)	

HERO Exercises
Happiness • Enthusiasm • Resilience • Optimism

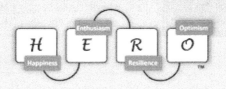

RESILIENT OPTIMISTS HAVE BETTER PHYSICAL HEALTH & BETTER RELATIONSHIPS

1. Resilience means the ability to bounce back from adversities. Write down 2 things about yourself that make you tough, and two skills you have used previously to overcome adversities. Remind yourself throughout the day that you genuinely possess these resilient traits.

    a. _____

    _____

    b. _____

    _____

2. Optimism often requires making a choice about how you view the world. Write down two positive things you want to happen tomorrow, and then spend a few minutes planning on how to make these optimistic attitudes/events a reality.

    a. _____

    _____

    b. _____

    _____

Please take time to review your previous HERO exercises. Research shows that reflecting on past thoughts about wellness further strengthens and solidifies your HERO wellness traits. The HERO exercises are intentionally repeated every 8 days because repetition is crucial to learning and incorporating new ideas.

Resilience is going to pay off.
~ Cat Zingano

Daily Journaling Form

EXERCISE	Exercise 30 minutes <u>at least 5 days</u> per week for 30 days, aim for at least moderate intensity

Type of Exercise		Duration	_____ minutes
Intensity	☐ Low	☐ Moderate	☐ High

MINDFULNESS	Practice mindfulness at least 10 minutes <u>at least 5 days</u> per week for 30 days

Today's Guided Meditation(s)	

SLEEP	Implement 4 or more of the 6 sleep hygiene practices <u>at least 5 days</u> per week for 30 days

Implemented These Sleep Hygiene Practices	☐ No electronics 90 min before bed	☐ Sleep mask or blackout shades	☐ Regular bedtime
	☐ No napping	☐ Warm bath/shower prior to bed	☐ Avoid caffeine 10 hrs before bed

SOCIAL CONNECTEDNESS	Meet or call at least two friends or family members <u>at least 5 days</u> per week for 30 days

	Friends		Family	
Today's Social Contacts	☐ Call	☐ In-person	☐ Call	☐ In-person

NUTRITION	Log your daily meals/snacks/beverages/alcohol <u>at least 5 days</u> per week for 30 days

Logged Meals/Snacks/Beverages/Alcohol	☐ Yes	☐ No
Strongly Recommended		
Implemented MIND Diet Principles	☐ Yes	☐ No
Practiced Mindful Meal Meditation	☐ Breakfast ☐ Lunch ☐ Dinner	

TODAY'S PROGRESS	
My Barrier(s)	
My Solution(s)	

HERO Exercises
Happiness • Enthusiasm • Resilience • Optimism

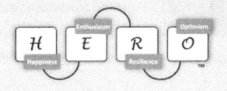

HAPPINESS & ENTHUSIASM ARE LINKED TO A STRONGER IMMUNE SYSTEM

1. In today's busy world, it's easy to overlook things that make us happy. Fast-paced lifestyles often become a barrier. Take a moment and mindfully reflect on your day, and write down two things that brought you happiness.

   a. _____

   _____

   b. _____

   _____

2. "Birds of a feather flock together," so surround yourself with happy and enthusiastic people. Write down the names of two people in your life that are happy and enthusiastic. Now, write down how and when you will connect with them.

   a. _____

   _____

   b. _____

   _____

Please take time to review your previous HERO exercises. Research shows that reflecting on past thoughts about wellness further strengthens and solidifies your HERO wellness traits. The HERO exercises are intentionally repeated every 8 days because repetition is crucial to learning and incorporating new ideas.

Years wrinkle the skin; but to give up enthusiasm wrinkles the soul.
~ *Douglas MacArthur*

Daily Journaling Form

EXERCISE	Exercise 30 minutes <u>at least 5 days</u> per week for 30 days, aim for at least moderate intensity		
Type of Exercise		Duration	_____ minutes
Intensity	☐ Low	☐ Moderate	☐ High

MINDFULNESS	Practice mindfulness at least 10 minutes <u>at least 5 days</u> per week for 30 days
Today's Guided Meditation(s)	

SLEEP	Implement 4 or more of the 6 sleep hygiene practices <u>at least 5 days</u> per week for 30 days		
Implemented These Sleep Hygiene Practices	☐ No electronics 90 min before bed	☐ Sleep mask or blackout shades	☐ Regular bedtime
	☐ No napping	☐ Warm bath/shower prior to bed	☐ Avoid caffeine 10 hrs before bed

SOCIAL CONNECTEDNESS	Meet or call at least two friends or family members <u>at least 5 days</u> per week for 30 days	
	Friends	Family
Today's Social Contacts	☐ Call ☐ In-person	☐ Call ☐ In-person

NUTRITION	Log your daily meals/snacks/beverages/alcohol <u>at least 5 days</u> per week for 30 days	
Logged Meals/Snacks/Beverages/Alcohol	☐ Yes	☐ No
Strongly Recommended		
Implemented MIND Diet Principles	☐ Yes	☐ No
Practiced Mindful Meal Meditation	☐ Breakfast ☐ Lunch ☐ Dinner	

TODAY'S PROGRESS	
My Barrier(s)	
My Solution(s)	

HERO Exercises
Happiness • Enthusiasm • Resilience • Optimism

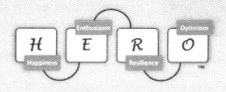

| RESILIENT & OPTIMISTIC PEOPLE REPORT BETTER MENTAL HEALTH & LIVE LONGER |

1. Dealing with life's challenges with humor builds resilience – the ability to bounce back from life's adversities. Write down two things that happened recently that you found humorous – things that made you smile or laugh.

   a. _____

   _____

   b. _____

   _____

2. Positive affirmations are a great way to build an optimistic mindset. Take a moment and write down two positive statements about yourself, your life, or your future. Purposefully remind yourself of these affirmations several times throughout your day.

   a. _____

   _____

   b. _____

   _____

Please take time to review your previous HERO exercises. Research shows that reflecting on past thoughts about wellness further strengthens and solidifies your HERO wellness traits. The HERO exercises are intentionally repeated every 8 days because repetition is crucial to learning and incorporating new ideas.

One small positive thought in the morning can change your whole day.
~ Anonymous

Daily Journaling Form

EXERCISE	Exercise 30 minutes at least 5 days per week for 30 days, aim for at least moderate intensity	
Type of Exercise		Duration _____ minutes
Intensity	☐ Low ☐ Moderate	☐ High

MINDFULNESS	Practice mindfulness at least 10 minutes at least 5 days per week for 30 days
Today's Guided Meditation(s)	

SLEEP	Implement 4 or more of the 6 sleep hygiene practices at least 5 days per week for 30 days		
Implemented These Sleep Hygiene Practices	☐ No electronics 90 min before bed	☐ Sleep mask or blackout shades	☐ Regular bedtime
	☐ No napping	☐ Warm bath/shower prior to bed	☐ Avoid caffeine 10 hrs before bed

SOCIAL CONNECTEDNESS	Meet or call at least two friends or family members at least 5 days per week for 30 days	
Today's Social Contacts	**Friends** ☐ Call ☐ In-person	**Family** ☐ Call ☐ In-person

NUTRITION	Log your daily meals/snacks/beverages/ alcohol at least 5 days per week for 30 days	
Logged Meals/Snacks/Beverages/Alcohol	☐ Yes	☐ No
Strongly Recommended		
Implemented MIND Diet Principles	☐ Yes	☐ No
Practiced Mindful Meal Meditation	☐ Breakfast ☐ Lunch ☐ Dinner	

TODAY'S PROGRESS	
My Barrier(s)	
My Solution(s)	

HERO Exercises
Happiness • Enthusiasm • Resilience • Optimism

HERO

HAPPINESS & ENTHUSIASM ARE KNOWN TO LESSEN PAIN

1. Random acts of kindness will increase your happiness! Take a moment and write down two random acts of kindness you will put into action today. If you don't have time to execute your plan today, be sure to make it happen first thing tomorrow morning.

    a. _____

    _____

    b. _____

    _____

2. When it comes to outlook, do you fall on the positive or the negative side of the fence? Having a positive attitude about life improves enthusiasm. To increase your enthusiasm, mindfully consider your day and write down two examples of your positive attitude and/or actions.

    a. _____

    _____

    b. _____

    _____

Please take time to review your previous HERO exercises. Research shows that reflecting on past thoughts about wellness further strengthens and solidifies your HERO wellness traits. The HERO exercises are intentionally repeated every 8 days because repetition is crucial to learning and incorporating new ideas.

To be happy you must be your own sunshine.
~ *C.E. Jerningham*

Daily Journaling Form

EXERCISE	Exercise 30 minutes <u>at least 5 days</u> per week for 30 days, aim for at least moderate intensity

Type of Exercise		Duration	_____ minutes
Intensity	☐ Low	☐ Moderate	☐ High

MINDFULNESS	Practice mindfulness at least 10 minutes <u>at least 5 days</u> per week for 30 days
Today's Guided Meditation(s)	

SLEEP	Implement 4 or more of the 6 sleep hygiene practices <u>at least 5 days</u> per week for 30 days

Implemented These Sleep Hygiene Practices	☐ No electronics 90 min before bed	☐ Sleep mask or blackout shades	☐ Regular bedtime
	☐ No napping	☐ Warm bath/shower prior to bed	☐ Avoid caffeine 10 hrs before bed

SOCIAL CONNECTEDNESS	Meet or call at least two friends or family members <u>at least 5 days</u> per week for 30 days

	Friends		Family	
Today's Social Contacts	☐ Call	☐ In-person	☐ Call	☐ In-person

NUTRITION	Log your daily meals/snacks/beverages/ alcohol <u>at least 5 days</u> per week for 30 days

Logged Meals/Snacks/Beverages/Alcohol	☐ Yes	☐ No
Strongly Recommended		
Implemented MIND Diet Principles	☐ Yes	☐ No
Practiced Mindful Meal Meditation	☐ Breakfast ☐ Lunch ☐ Dinner	

TODAY'S PROGRESS	
My Barrier(s)	
My Solution(s)	

HERO Exercises
Happiness • Enthusiasm • Resilience • Optimism

HERO

RESILIENCE & OPTIMISM FERTILIZE A POSITIVE ATTITUDE

1. Being of service to others is a great way to build resilience. List two things you did today (or will do tomorrow) to give back to others or to brighten their day.

   a. _____

   _____

   b. _____

   _____

2. Is your glass half-full or half-empty? How you view the world matters! Write down two things that happened today that you viewed as negative. Take a moment and give this some thought, and then write down a less negative, or even a positive interpretation of the same events.

   a. _____

   _____

   b. _____

   _____

Please take time to review your previous HERO exercises. Research shows that reflecting on past thoughts about wellness further strengthens and solidifies your HERO wellness traits. The HERO exercises are intentionally repeated every 8 days because repetition is crucial to learning and incorporating new ideas.

Don't put the key to your happiness in somebody else's pocket.
~ Anonymous

Daily Journaling Form

EXERCISE	Exercise 30 minutes <u>at least 5 days</u> per week for 30 days, aim for at least moderate intensity	
Type of Exercise		**Duration** _____ minutes
Intensity	☐ Low ☐ Moderate	☐ High

MINDFULNESS	Practice mindfulness at least 10 minutes <u>at least 5 days</u> per week for 30 days
Today's Guided Meditation(s)	

SLEEP	Implement 4 or more of the 6 sleep hygiene practices <u>at least 5 days</u> per week for 30 days		
Implemented These Sleep Hygiene Practices	☐ No electronics 90 min before bed	☐ Sleep mask or blackout shades	☐ Regular bedtime
	☐ No napping	☐ Warm bath/shower prior to bed	☐ Avoid caffeine 10 hrs before bed

SOCIAL CONNECTEDNESS	Meet or call at least two friends or family members <u>at least 5 days</u> per week for 30 days	
	Friends	**Family**
Today's Social Contacts	☐ Call ☐ In-person	☐ Call ☐ In-person

NUTRITION	Log your daily meals/snacks/beverages/ alcohol <u>at least 5 days</u> per week for 30 days		
Logged Meals/Snacks/Beverages/Alcohol	☐ Yes		☐ No
Strongly Recommended			
Implemented MIND Diet Principles	☐ Yes		☐ No
Practiced Mindful Meal Meditation	☐ Breakfast	☐ Lunch	☐ Dinner

TODAY'S PROGRESS	
My Barrier(s)	
My Solution(s)	

HERO Exercises
Happiness • Enthusiasm • Resilience • Optimism

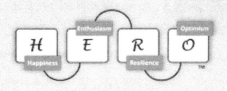

HAPPINESS & ENTHUSIASM PREDICT LOWER HEART RATE & BLOOD PRESSURE

1. Thinking about happy memories can positively impact your level of happiness! Write down two memories that bring a smile to your face. Next, spend a few minutes reliving each of these happy memories, and watch your current level of happiness increase.

    a. _____

    _____

    b. _____

    _____

2. Gratitude is known to increase feelings of happiness and enthusiasm. To increase these feelings, mindfully consider your day and write down two examples of things that happened today that increased your feelings of gratitude.

    a. _____

    _____

    b. _____

    _____

Please take time to review your previous HERO exercises. Research shows that reflecting on past thoughts about wellness further strengthens and solidifies your HERO wellness traits. The HERO exercises are intentionally repeated every 8 days because repetition is crucial to learning and incorporating new ideas.

Talent without enthusiasm is like a Ferrari without fuel.
~ Sebastyne Young

Daily Journaling Form

EXERCISE	Exercise 30 minutes <u>at least 5 days</u> per week for 30 days, aim for at least moderate intensity

Type of Exercise		Duration	_____ minutes
Intensity	☐ Low	☐ Moderate	☐ High

MINDFULNESS	Practice mindfulness at least 10 minutes <u>at least 5 days</u> per week for 30 days
Today's Guided Meditation(s)	

SLEEP	Implement 4 or more of the 6 sleep hygiene practices <u>at least 5 days</u> per week for 30 days

Implemented These Sleep Hygiene Practices	☐ No electronics 90 min before bed	☐ Sleep mask or blackout shades	☐ Regular bedtime
	☐ No napping	☐ Warm bath/shower prior to bed	☐ Avoid caffeine 10 hrs before bed

SOCIAL CONNECTEDNESS	Meet or call at least two friends or family members <u>at least 5 days</u> per week for 30 days

	Friends		Family	
Today's Social Contacts	☐	☐	☐	☐
	Call	In-person	Call	In-person

NUTRITION	Log your daily meals/snacks/beverages/ alcohol <u>at least 5 days</u> per week for 30 days

Logged Meals/Snacks/Beverages/Alcohol	☐ Yes	☐ No
Strongly Recommended		
Implemented MIND Diet Principles	☐ Yes	☐ No
Practiced Mindful Meal Meditation	☐ Breakfast ☐ Lunch ☐ Dinner	

TODAY'S PROGRESS	
My Barrier(s)	
My Solution(s)	

HERO Exercises
Happiness • Enthusiasm • Resilience • Optimism

RESILIENCE & OPTIMISM ARE LINKED TO GREATER LIFE SATISFACTION

1. People are quick to point out faults and weaknesses. Acknowledging others' successes is a great way to build and strengthen your resilience while making another person feel great. Think of two people that have recently achieved some type of success, personal or work-related, and write down how you plan to acknowledge their achievement.

   a. _____

   _____

   b. _____

   _____

2. Have you heard of *Paying it Forward*? Someone does something kind for you and you pass it forward by doing something kind for another. Write down two times others have done something kind for you and how that made you feel. Make a plan to pass along those acts of kindness and brighten someone else's day.

   a. _____

   _____

   b. _____

   _____

Please take time to review your previous HERO exercises. Research shows that reflecting on past thoughts about wellness further strengthens and solidifies your HERO wellness traits. The HERO exercises are intentionally repeated every 8 days because repetition is crucial to learning and incorporating new ideas.

I am an optimist. It does not seem too much use being anything else.
~ *Winston Churchill*

Daily Journaling Form

EXERCISE	Exercise 30 minutes <u>at least 5 days</u> per week for 30 days, aim for at least moderate intensity

Type of Exercise		Duration	_____ minutes
Intensity	☐ Low	☐ Moderate	☐ High

MINDFULNESS	Practice mindfulness at least 10 minutes <u>at least 5 days</u> per week for 30 days

Today's Guided Meditation(s)	

SLEEP	Implement 4 or more of the 6 sleep hygiene practices <u>at least 5 days</u> per week for 30 days

Implemented These Sleep Hygiene Practices	☐ No electronics 90 min before bed	☐ Sleep mask or blackout shades	☐ Regular bedtime
	☐ No napping	☐ Warm bath/shower prior to bed	☐ Avoid caffeine 10 hrs before bed

SOCIAL CONNECTEDNESS	Meet or call at least two friends or family members <u>at least 5 days</u> per week for 30 days

Today's Social Contacts	Friends		Family	
	☐ Call	☐ In-person	☐ Call	☐ In-person

NUTRITION	Log your daily meals/snacks/beverages/ alcohol <u>at least 5 days</u> per week for 30 days

Logged Meals/Snacks/Beverages/Alcohol	☐ Yes	☐ No
Strongly Recommended		
Implemented MIND Diet Principles	☐ Yes	☐ No
Practiced Mindful Meal Meditation	☐ Breakfast ☐ Lunch ☐ Dinner	

TODAY'S PROGRESS	
My Barrier(s)	
My Solution(s)	

HERO Exercises
Happiness • Enthusiasm • Resilience • Optimism

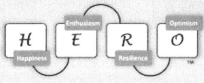

HAPPINESS & ENTHUSIASM ARE LINKED TO LONGEVITY

1. To increase your happiness, let's work on strengthening your happiness muscle. Take a moment and write down two positive things that you'd like to experience today. Also, two to three times today, find a few minutes to visualize and relish these positive experiences.

   a. _____

   _____

   b. _____

   _____

2. Having a goal or a project that inspires you will increase your enthusiasm. Write down two projects you find inspiring and set a start date. Put the date on your calendar with reminder alerts – make it happen and watch your enthusiasm improve!

   a. _____

   _____

   b. _____

   _____

Please take time to review your previous HERO exercises. Research shows that reflecting on past thoughts about wellness further strengthens and solidifies your HERO wellness traits. The HERO exercises are intentionally repeated every 8 days because repetition is crucial to learning and incorporating new ideas.

Remember happiness is a way of travel not a destination.
~ Anonymous

Daily Journaling Form

EXERCISE	Exercise 30 minutes <u>at least 5 days</u> per week for 30 days, aim for at least moderate intensity	
Type of Exercise		**Duration** _____ minutes
Intensity	☐ Low	☐ Moderate ☐ High

MINDFULNESS	Practice mindfulness at least 10 minutes <u>at least 5 days</u> per week for 30 days
Today's Guided Meditation(s)	

SLEEP	Implement 4 or more of the 6 sleep hygiene practices <u>at least 5 days</u> per week for 30 days		
Implemented These Sleep Hygiene Practices	☐ No electronics 90 min before bed	☐ Sleep mask or blackout shades	☐ Regular bedtime
	☐ No napping	☐ Warm bath/shower prior to bed	☐ Avoid caffeine 10 hrs before bed

SOCIAL CONNECTEDNESS	Meet or call at least two friends or family members <u>at least 5 days</u> per week for 30 days	
	Friends	**Family**
Today's Social Contacts	☐ Call ☐ In-person	☐ Call ☐ In-person

NUTRITION	Log your daily meals/snacks/beverages/alcohol <u>at least 5 days</u> per week for 30 days	
Logged Meals/Snacks/Beverages/Alcohol	☐ Yes	☐ No
Strongly Recommended		
Implemented MIND Diet Principles	☐ Yes	☐ No
Practiced Mindful Meal Meditation	☐ Breakfast ☐ Lunch ☐ Dinner	

TODAY'S PROGRESS	
My Barrier(s)	
My Solution(s)	

HERO Exercises
*H*appiness • *E*nthusiasm • *R*esilience • *O*ptimism

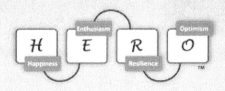

RESILIENT OPTIMISTS HAVE BETTER PHYSICAL HEALTH & BETTER RELATIONSHIPS

1. Resilience means the ability to bounce back from adversities. Write down 2 things about yourself that make you tough, and two skills you have used previously to overcome adversities. Remind yourself throughout the day that you genuinely possess these resilient traits.

     a. _____

         _____

     b. _____

         _____

2. Optimism often requires making a choice about how you view the world. Write down two positive things you want to happen tomorrow, and then spend a few minutes planning on how to make these optimistic attitudes/events a reality.

     a. _____

         _____

     b. _____

         _____

Please take time to review your previous HERO exercises. Research shows that reflecting on past thoughts about wellness further strengthens and solidifies your HERO wellness traits. The HERO exercises are intentionally repeated every 8 days because repetition is crucial to learning and incorporating new ideas.

People tend to overstate my resilience, but, of course, I hope they're right.
~ *David Brudnoy*

Daily Journaling Form

EXERCISE	Exercise 30 minutes <u>at least 5 days</u> per week for 30 days, aim for at least moderate intensity

Type of Exercise		Duration	_____ minutes
Intensity	☐ Low	☐ Moderate	☐ High

MINDFULNESS	Practice mindfulness at least 10 minutes <u>at least 5 days</u> per week for 30 days
Today's Guided Meditation(s)	

SLEEP	Implement 4 or more of the 6 sleep hygiene practices <u>at least 5 days</u> per week for 30 days

Implemented These Sleep Hygiene Practices	☐ No electronics 90 min before bed	☐ Sleep mask or blackout shades	☐ Regular bedtime
	☐ No napping	☐ Warm bath/shower prior to bed	☐ Avoid caffeine 10 hrs before bed

SOCIAL CONNECTEDNESS	Meet or call at least two friends or family members <u>at least 5 days</u> per week for 30 days

	Friends		Family	
Today's Social Contacts	☐ Call	☐ In-person	☐ Call	☐ In-person

NUTRITION	Log your daily meals/snacks/beverages/ alcohol <u>at least 5 days</u> per week for 30 days

Logged Meals/Snacks/Beverages/Alcohol	☐ Yes	☐ No
Strongly Recommended		
Implemented MIND Diet Principles	☐ Yes	☐ No
Practiced Mindful Meal Meditation	☐ Breakfast ☐ Lunch ☐ Dinner	

TODAY'S PROGRESS	
My Barrier(s)	
My Solution(s)	

HERO Exercises
*H*appiness • *E*nthusiasm • *R*esilience • *O*ptimism

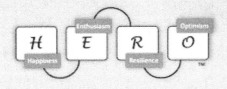

HAPPINESS & ENTHUSIASM ARE LINKED TO A STRONGER IMMUNE SYSTEM

1. In today's busy world, it's easy to overlook things that make us happy. Fast-paced lifestyles often become a barrier. Take a moment and mindfully reflect on your day, and write down two things that brought you happiness.

   a. _____

   _____

   b. _____

   _____

2. "Birds of a feather flock together," so surround yourself with happy and enthusiastic people. Write down the names of two people in your life that are happy and enthusiastic. Now, write down how and when you will connect with them.

   a. _____

   _____

   b. _____

   _____

Please take time to review your previous HERO exercises. Research shows that reflecting on past thoughts about wellness further strengthens and solidifies your HERO wellness traits. The HERO exercises are intentionally repeated every 8 days because repetition is crucial to learning and incorporating new ideas.

If you want to be happy, be.
~ Leo Tolstoy

Daily Journaling Form

EXERCISE	Exercise 30 minutes <u>at least 5 days</u> per week for 30 days, aim for at least moderate intensity		
Type of Exercise		Duration	_____ minutes
Intensity	☐ Low	☐ Moderate	☐ High

MINDFULNESS	Practice mindfulness at least 10 minutes <u>at least 5 days</u> per week for 30 days
Today's Guided Meditation(s)	

SLEEP	Implement 4 or more of the 6 sleep hygiene practices <u>at least 5 days</u> per week for 30 days		
Implemented These Sleep Hygiene Practices	☐ No electronics 90 min before bed	☐ Sleep mask or blackout shades	☐ Regular bedtime
	☐ No napping	☐ Warm bath/shower prior to bed	☐ Avoid caffeine 10 hrs before bed

SOCIAL CONNECTEDNESS	Meet or call at least two friends or family members <u>at least 5 days</u> per week for 30 days	
Today's Social Contacts	**Friends** ☐ Call ☐ In-person	**Family** ☐ Call ☐ In-person

NUTRITION	Log your daily meals/snacks/beverages/ alcohol <u>at least 5 days</u> per week for 30 days	
Logged Meals/Snacks/Beverages/Alcohol	☐ Yes	☐ No
Strongly Recommended		
Implemented MIND Diet Principles	☐ Yes	☐ No
Practiced Mindful Meal Meditation	☐ Breakfast ☐ Lunch ☐ Dinner	

TODAY'S PROGRESS	
My Barrier(s)	
My Solution(s)	

HERO Exercises
*H*appiness • *E*nthusiasm • *R*esilience • *O*ptimism

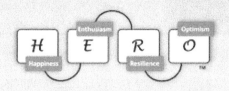

RESILIENT & OPTIMISTIC PEOPLE REPORT BETTER MENTAL HEALTH & LIVE LONGER

1. Dealing with life's challenges with humor builds resilience – the ability to bounce back from life's adversities. Write down two things that happened recently that you found humorous – things that made you smile or laugh.

   a. _____

   _____

   b. _____

   _____

2. Positive affirmations are a great way to build an optimistic mindset. Take a moment and write down two positive statements about yourself, your life, or your future. Purposefully remind yourself of these affirmations several times throughout your day.

   a. _____

   _____

   b. _____

   _____

Please take time to review your previous HERO exercises. Research shows that reflecting on past thoughts about wellness further strengthens and solidifies your HERO wellness traits. The HERO exercises are intentionally repeated every 8 days because repetition is crucial to learning and incorporating new ideas.

Life doesn't get easier or more forgiving; we get stronger and more resilient.
~ Dr. Steve Maraboli

Daily Journaling Form

EXERCISE	Exercise 30 minutes <u>at least 5 days</u> per week for 30 days, aim for at least moderate intensity

Type of Exercise		Duration	_____ minutes
Intensity	☐ Low	☐ Moderate	☐ High

MINDFULNESS	Practice mindfulness at least 10 minutes <u>at least 5 days</u> per week for 30 days

Today's Guided Meditation(s)	

SLEEP	Implement 4 or more of the 6 sleep hygiene practices <u>at least 5 days</u> per week for 30 days

Implemented These Sleep Hygiene Practices	☐ No electronics 90 min before bed	☐ Sleep mask or blackout shades	☐ Regular bedtime
	☐ No napping	☐ Warm bath/shower prior to bed	☐ Avoid caffeine 10 hrs before bed

SOCIAL CONNECTEDNESS	Meet or call at least two friends or family members <u>at least 5 days</u> per week for 30 days

Today's Social Contacts	Friends		Family	
	☐ Call	☐ In-person	☐ Call	☐ In-person

NUTRITION	Log your daily meals/snacks/beverages/ alcohol <u>at least 5 days</u> per week for 30 days

Logged Meals/Snacks/Beverages/Alcohol	☐ Yes	☐ No
Strongly Recommended		
Implemented MIND Diet Principles	☐ Yes	☐ No
Practiced Mindful Meal Meditation	☐ Breakfast ☐ Lunch ☐ Dinner	

TODAY'S PROGRESS	
My Barrier(s)	
My Solution(s)	

HERO Exercises
*H*appiness • *E*nthusiasm • *R*esilience • *O*ptimism

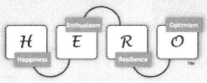

HAPPINESS & ENTHUSIASM ARE KNOWN TO LESSEN PAIN

1. Random acts of kindness will increase your happiness! Take a moment and write down two random acts of kindness you will put into action today. If you don't have time to execute your plan today, be sure to make it happen first thing tomorrow morning.

   a. _____

   _____

   b. _____

   _____

2. When it comes to outlook, do you fall on the positive or the negative side of the fence? Having a positive attitude about life improves enthusiasm. To increase your enthusiasm, mindfully consider your day and write down two examples of your positive attitude and/or actions.

   a. _____

   _____

   b. _____

   _____

Please take time to review your previous HERO exercises. Research shows that reflecting on past thoughts about wellness further strengthens and solidifies your HERO wellness traits. The HERO exercises are intentionally repeated every 8 days because repetition is crucial to learning and incorporating new ideas.

A mediocre idea that generates enthusiasm will go farther
than a great idea that inspires no one.

~ *Mary Kay Ash*

Daily Journaling Form

EXERCISE	Exercise 30 minutes <u>at least 5 days</u> per week for 30 days, aim for at least moderate intensity

Type of Exercise		Duration	_____ minutes
Intensity	☐ Low	☐ Moderate	☐ High

MINDFULNESS	Practice mindfulness at least 10 minutes <u>at least 5 days</u> per week for 30 days

Today's Guided Meditation(s)	

SLEEP	Implement 4 or more of the 6 sleep hygiene practices <u>at least 5 days</u> per week for 30 days

Implemented These Sleep Hygiene Practices	☐ No electronics 90 min before bed	☐ Sleep mask or blackout shades	☐ Regular bedtime
	☐ No napping	☐ Warm bath/shower prior to bed	☐ Avoid caffeine 10 hrs before bed

SOCIAL CONNECTEDNESS	Meet or call at least two friends or family members <u>at least 5 days</u> per week for 30 days

Today's Social Contacts	Friends		Family	
	☐ Call	☐ In-person	☐ Call	☐ In-person

NUTRITION	Log your daily meals/snacks/beverages/ alcohol <u>at least 5 days</u> per week for 30 days

Logged Meals/Snacks/Beverages/Alcohol	☐ Yes	☐ No
Strongly Recommended		
Implemented MIND Diet Principles	☐ Yes	☐ No
Practiced Mindful Meal Meditation	☐ Breakfast ☐ Lunch	☐ Dinner

TODAY'S PROGRESS	
My Barrier(s)	
My Solution(s)	

HERO Exercises
*H*appiness • *E*nthusiasm • *R*esilience • *O*ptimism

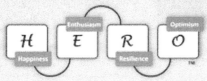

RESILIENCE & OPTIMISM FERTILIZE A POSITIVE ATTITUDE

1. Being of service to others is a great way to build resilience. List two things you did today (or will do tomorrow) to give back to others or to brighten their day.

   a. _____

   _____

   b. _____

   _____

2. Is your glass half-full or half-empty? How you view the world matters! Write down two things that happened today that you viewed as negative. Take a moment and give this some thought, and then write down a less negative, or even a positive interpretation of the same events.

   a. _____

   _____

   b. _____

   _____

Please take time to review your previous HERO exercises. Research shows that reflecting on past thoughts about wellness further strengthens and solidifies your HERO wellness traits. The HERO exercises are intentionally repeated every 8 days because repetition is crucial to learning and incorporating new ideas.

When faced with a challenge, look for a way, not a way out.
~ David L. Weatherford

Daily Journaling Form

EXERCISE	Exercise 30 minutes <u>at least 5 days</u> per week for 30 days, aim for at least moderate intensity

Type of Exercise		Duration	_____ minutes
Intensity	☐ Low	☐ Moderate	☐ High

MINDFULNESS	Practice mindfulness at least 10 minutes <u>at least 5 days</u> per week for 30 days

Today's Guided Meditation(s)	

SLEEP	Implement 4 or more of the 6 sleep hygiene practices <u>at least 5 days</u> per week for 30 days

Implemented These Sleep Hygiene Practices	☐ No electronics 90 min before bed	☐ Sleep mask or blackout shades	☐ Regular bedtime
	☐ No napping	☐ Warm bath/shower prior to bed	☐ Avoid caffeine 10 hrs before bed

SOCIAL CONNECTEDNESS	Meet or call at least two friends or family members <u>at least 5 days</u> per week for 30 days

	Friends		Family	
Today's Social Contacts	☐ Call	☐ In-person	☐ Call	☐ In-person

NUTRITION	Log your daily meals/snacks/beverages/ alcohol <u>at least 5 days</u> per week for 30 days

Logged Meals/Snacks/Beverages/Alcohol	☐ Yes	☐ No
Strongly Recommended		
Implemented MIND Diet Principles	☐ Yes	☐ No
Practiced Mindful Meal Meditation	☐ Breakfast ☐ Lunch	☐ Dinner

TODAY'S PROGRESS	
My Barrier(s)	
My Solution(s)	

HERO Exercises
Happiness • Enthusiasm • Resilience • Optimism

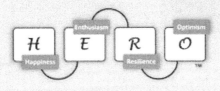

HAPPINESS & ENTHUSIASM PREDICT LOWER HEART RATE & BLOOD PRESSURE

1. Thinking about happy memories can positively impact your level of happiness! Write down two memories that bring a smile to your face. Next, spend a few minutes reliving each of these happy memories, and watch your current level of happiness increase.

   a. _____

   _____

   b. _____

   _____

2. Gratitude is known to increase feelings of happiness and enthusiasm. To increase these feelings, mindfully consider your day and write down two examples of things that happened today that increased your feelings of gratitude.

   a. _____

   _____

   b. _____

   _____

Please take time to review your previous HERO exercises. Research shows that reflecting on past thoughts about wellness further strengthens and solidifies your HERO wellness traits. The HERO exercises are intentionally repeated every 8 days because repetition is crucial to learning and incorporating new ideas.

Pessimism leads to weakness, optimism to power.
~ *William James*

Daily Journaling Form

EXERCISE	Exercise 30 minutes <u>at least 5 days</u> per week for 30 days, aim for at least moderate intensity		
Type of Exercise		Duration	_____ minutes
Intensity	☐ Low	☐ Moderate	☐ High

MINDFULNESS	Practice mindfulness at least 10 minutes <u>at least 5 days</u> per week for 30 days
Today's Guided Meditation(s)	

SLEEP	Implement 4 or more of the 6 sleep hygiene practices <u>at least 5 days</u> per week for 30 days		
Implemented These Sleep Hygiene Practices	☐ No electronics 90 min before bed	☐ Sleep mask or blackout shades	☐ Regular bedtime
	☐ No napping	☐ Warm bath/shower prior to bed	☐ Avoid caffeine 10 hrs before bed

SOCIAL CONNECTEDNESS	Meet or call at least two friends or family members <u>at least 5 days</u> per week for 30 days			
	Friends		Family	
Today's Social Contacts	☐ Call	☐ In-person	☐ Call	☐ In-person

NUTRITION	Log your daily meals/snacks/beverages/ alcohol <u>at least 5 days</u> per week for 30 days		
Logged Meals/Snacks/Beverages/Alcohol	☐ Yes		☐ No
Strongly Recommended			
Implemented MIND Diet Principles	☐ Yes		☐ No
Practiced Mindful Meal Meditation	☐ Breakfast	☐ Lunch	☐ Dinner

TODAY'S PROGRESS	
My Barrier(s)	
My Solution(s)	

HERO Exercises
Happiness • Enthusiasm • Resilience • Optimism

RESILIENCE & OPTIMISM ARE LINKED TO GREATER LIFE SATISFACTION

---

1. People are quick to point out faults and weaknesses. Acknowledging others' successes is a great way to build and strengthen your resilience while making another person feel great. Think of two people that have recently achieved some type of success, personal or work-related, and write down how you plan to acknowledge their achievement.

   a. _____

   _____

   b. _____

   _____

2. Have you heard of *Paying it Forward*? Someone does something kind for you and you pass it forward by doing something kind for another. Write down two times others have done something kind for you and how that made you feel. Make a plan to pass along those acts of kindness and brighten someone else's day.

   a. _____

   _____

   b. _____

   _____

Please take time to review your previous HERO exercises. Research shows that reflecting on past thoughts about wellness further strengthens and solidifies your HERO wellness traits. The HERO exercises are intentionally repeated every 8 days because repetition is crucial to learning and incorporating new ideas.

Resilience: facing down rejection & criticism on the road to success.
~ *Mark McGuinness*

Daily Journaling Form

EXERCISE	Exercise 30 minutes <u>at least 5 days</u> per week for 30 days, aim for at least moderate intensity

Type of Exercise		Duration	_____ minutes
Intensity	☐ Low	☐ Moderate	☐ High

MINDFULNESS	Practice mindfulness at least 10 minutes <u>at least 5 days</u> per week for 30 days

Today's Guided Meditation(s)	

SLEEP	Implement 4 or more of the 6 sleep hygiene practices <u>at least 5 days</u> per week for 30 days

Implemented These Sleep Hygiene Practices	☐ No electronics 90 min before bed	☐ Sleep mask or blackout shades	☐ Regular bedtime
	☐ No napping	☐ Warm bath/shower prior to bed	☐ Avoid caffeine 10 hrs before bed

SOCIAL CONNECTEDNESS	Meet or call at least two friends or family members <u>at least 5 days</u> per week for 30 days

Today's Social Contacts	**Friends**		**Family**	
	☐ Call	☐ In-person	☐ Call	☐ In-person

NUTRITION	Log your daily meals/snacks/beverages/ alcohol <u>at least 5 days</u> per week for 30 days

Logged Meals/Snacks/Beverages/Alcohol	☐ Yes	☐ No
Strongly Recommended		
Implemented MIND Diet Principles	☐ Yes	☐ No
Practiced Mindful Meal Meditation	☐ Breakfast ☐ Lunch ☐ Dinner	

TODAY'S PROGRESS	
My Barrier(s)	
My Solution(s)	

HERO Exercises
Happiness • Enthusiasm • Resilience • Optimism

HAPPINESS & ENTHUSIASM ARE LINKED TO LONGEVITY

1. To increase your happiness, let's work on strengthening your happiness muscle. Take a moment and write down two positive things that you'd like to experience today. Also, two to three times today, find a few minutes to visualize and relish these positive experiences.

   a. _____

   _____

   b. _____

   _____

2. Having a goal or a project that inspires you will increase your enthusiasm. Write down two projects you find inspiring and set a start date. Put the date on your calendar with reminder alerts – make it happen and watch your enthusiasm improve!

   a. _____

   _____

   b. _____

   _____

Please take time to review your previous HERO exercises. Research shows that reflecting on past thoughts about wellness further strengthens and solidifies your HERO wellness traits. The HERO exercises are intentionally repeated every 8 days because repetition is crucial to learning and incorporating new ideas.

For every minute you are angry you lose sixty seconds of happiness.
~ *Ralph Waldo Emerson*

Daily Journaling Form

EXERCISE	Exercise 30 minutes <u>at least 5 days</u> per week for 30 days, aim for at least moderate intensity

Type of Exercise		Duration	_____ minutes
Intensity	☐ Low	☐ Moderate	☐ High

MINDFULNESS	Practice mindfulness at least 10 minutes <u>at least 5 days</u> per week for 30 days

Today's Guided Meditation(s)	

SLEEP	Implement 4 or more of the 6 sleep hygiene practices <u>at least 5 days</u> per week for 30 days

Implemented These Sleep Hygiene Practices	☐ No electronics 90 min before bed	☐ Sleep mask or blackout shades	☐ Regular bedtime
	☐ No napping	☐ Warm bath/shower prior to bed	☐ Avoid caffeine 10 hrs before bed

SOCIAL CONNECTEDNESS	Meet or call at least two friends or family members <u>at least 5 days</u> per week for 30 days

	Friends		Family	
Today's Social Contacts	☐ Call	☐ In-person	☐ Call	☐ In-person

NUTRITION	Log your daily meals/snacks/beverages/ alcohol <u>at least 5 days</u> per week for 30 days

Logged Meals/Snacks/Beverages/Alcohol	☐ Yes	☐ No
Strongly Recommended		
Implemented MIND Diet Principles	☐ Yes	☐ No
Practiced Mindful Meal Meditation	☐ Breakfast ☐ Lunch	☐ Dinner

TODAY'S PROGRESS	
My Barrier(s)	
My Solution(s)	

HERO Exercises
*H*appiness • *E*nthusiasm • *R*esilience • *O*ptimism

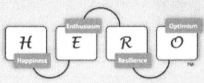

RESILIENT OPTIMISTS HAVE BETTER PHYSICAL HEALTH & BETTER RELATIONSHIPS

---

1. Resilience means the ability to bounce back from adversities. Write down 2 things about yourself that make you tough, and two skills you have used previously to overcome adversities. Remind yourself throughout the day that you genuinely possess these resilient traits.

    a. _____

    _____

    b. _____

    _____

2. Optimism often requires making a choice about how you view the world. Write down two positive things you want to happen tomorrow, and then spend a few minutes planning on how to make these optimistic attitudes/events a reality.

    a. _____

    _____

    b. _____

    _____

Please take time to review your previous HERO exercises. Research shows that reflecting on past thoughts about wellness further strengthens and solidifies your HERO wellness traits. The HERO exercises are intentionally repeated every 8 days because repetition is crucial to learning and incorporating new ideas.

Resilience is based on compassion for ourselves as well as compassion for others.
~ *Sharon Salzberg*

Daily Journaling Form

EXERCISE	Exercise 30 minutes <u>at least 5 days</u> per week for 30 days, aim for at least moderate intensity

Type of Exercise		Duration	_____ minutes
Intensity	☐ Low	☐ Moderate	☐ High

MINDFULNESS	Practice mindfulness at least 10 minutes <u>at least 5 days</u> per week for 30 days

Today's Guided Meditation(s)	

SLEEP	Implement 4 or more of the 6 sleep hygiene practices <u>at least 5 days</u> per week for 30 days

Implemented These Sleep Hygiene Practices	☐ No electronics 90 min before bed	☐ Sleep mask or blackout shades	☐ Regular bedtime
	☐ No napping	☐ Warm bath/shower prior to bed	☐ Avoid caffeine 10 hrs before bed

SOCIAL CONNECTEDNESS	Meet or call at least two friends or family members <u>at least 5 days</u> per week for 30 days

	Friends		Family	
Today's Social Contacts	☐ Call	☐ In-person	☐ Call	☐ In-person

NUTRITION	Log your daily meals/snacks/beverages/ alcohol <u>at least 5 days</u> per week for 30 days

Logged Meals/Snacks/Beverages/Alcohol	☐ Yes	☐ No
Strongly Recommended		
Implemented MIND Diet Principles	☐ Yes	☐ No
Practiced Mindful Meal Meditation	☐ Breakfast ☐ Lunch	☐ Dinner

TODAY'S PROGRESS	
My Barrier(s)	
My Solution(s)	

HERO Exercises
Happiness • Enthusiasm • Resilience • Optimism

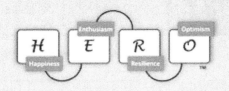

HAPPINESS & ENTHUSIASM ARE LINKED TO A STRONGER IMMUNE SYSTEM

1. In today's busy world, it's easy to overlook things that make us happy. Fast-paced lifestyles often become a barrier. Take a moment and mindfully reflect on your day, and write down two things that brought you happiness.

   a. _____

   _____

   b. _____

   _____

2. "Birds of a feather flock together," so surround yourself with happy and enthusiastic people. Write down the names of two people in your life that are happy and enthusiastic. Now, write down how and when you will connect with them.

   a. _____

   _____

   b. _____

   _____

Please take time to review your previous HERO exercises. Research shows that reflecting on past thoughts about wellness further strengthens and solidifies your HERO wellness traits. The HERO exercises are intentionally repeated every 8 days because repetition is crucial to learning and incorporating new ideas.

We're just enthusiastic about what we do.
~ *Steve Jobs*

Daily Journaling Form

EXERCISE	Exercise 30 minutes at least 5 days per week for 30 days, aim for at least moderate intensity	
Type of Exercise		Duration _____ minutes
Intensity	☐ Low ☐ Moderate ☐ High	

MINDFULNESS	Practice mindfulness at least 10 minutes at least 5 days per week for 30 days
Today's Guided Meditation(s)	

SLEEP	Implement 4 or more of the 6 sleep hygiene practices at least 5 days per week for 30 days		
Implemented These Sleep Hygiene Practices	☐ No electronics 90 min before bed	☐ Sleep mask or blackout shades	☐ Regular bedtime
	☐ No napping	☐ Warm bath/shower prior to bed	☐ Avoid caffeine 10 hrs before bed

SOCIAL CONNECTEDNESS	Meet or call at least two friends or family members at least 5 days per week for 30 days	
Today's Social Contacts	Friends ☐ Call ☐ In-person	Family ☐ Call ☐ In-person

NUTRITION	Log your daily meals/snacks/beverages/ alcohol at least 5 days per week for 30 days	
Logged Meals/Snacks/Beverages/Alcohol	☐ Yes	☐ No
Strongly Recommended		
Implemented MIND Diet Principles	☐ Yes	☐ No
Practiced Mindful Meal Meditation	☐ Breakfast ☐ Lunch ☐ Dinner	

TODAY'S PROGRESS	
My Barrier(s)	
My Solution(s)	

HERO Exercises
Happiness • Enthusiasm • Resilience • Optimism

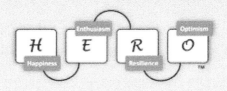

| RESILIENT & OPTIMISTIC PEOPLE REPORT BETTER MENTAL HEALTH & LIVE LONGER |

1. Dealing with life's challenges with humor builds resilience – the ability to bounce back from life's adversities. Write down two things that happened recently that you found humorous – things that made you smile or laugh.

    a. _____

    _____

    b. _____

    _____

2. Positive affirmations are a great way to build an optimistic mindset. Take a moment and write down two positive statements about yourself, your life, or your future. Purposefully remind yourself of these affirmations several times throughout your day.

    a. _____

    _____

    b. _____

    _____

Please take time to review your previous HERO exercises. Research shows that reflecting on past thoughts about wellness further strengthens and solidifies your HERO wellness traits. The HERO exercises are intentionally repeated every 8 days because repetition is crucial to learning and incorporating new ideas.

Resilience is all about being able to overcome the unexpected.
~ Jamais Cascio

HERO Wellness Scale

Day 60

Before you begin Phase 3 of the program, please complete the *HERO Wellness Scale* on the following page. Comparing your Day 1, Day 30 and Day 60 HERO scores will allow you to measure the progress you've made during the first 60 days of the program.

Please don't underestimate the value of using the *HERO Wellness Scale*, as the feedback will be both useful and motivational.

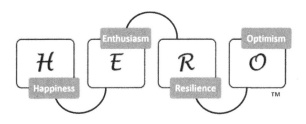

COMPLETE ON DAY 60

DATE: _____

HERO WELLNESS SCALE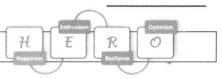

Please circle ONE NUMBER for each question below.

1. On average, during the last 7 DAYS, how happy have you felt?

0	1	2	3	4	5	6	7	8	9	10
Not at all happy		Mildly happy			Moderately happy			Highly happy		Extremely happy

2. On average, during the last 7 DAYS, how enthusiastic have you felt?

0	1	2	3	4	5	6	7	8	9	10
Not at all enthusiastic		Mildly enthusiastic		Moderately enthusiastic				Highly enthusiastic		Extremely enthusiastic

3. On average, during the last 7 DAYS, how resilient have you felt?

0	1	2	3	4	5	6	7	8	9	10
Not at all resilient		Mildly resilient			Moderately resilient			Highly resilient		Extremely resilient

4. On average, during the last 7 DAYS, how optimistic have you felt?

0	1	2	3	4	5	6	7	8	9	10
Not at all optimistic		Mildly optimistic			Moderately optimistic			Highly optimistic		Extremely optimistic

5. On average, during the last 7 DAYS, how would you rate your mental wellness?

0	1	2	3	4	5	6	7	8	9	10
Not at all good		Mildly good			Moderately good			Markedly good		Extremely good

- -

SCORING: To calculate total score, add all circled numbers.

TOTAL SCORE: 0 - 50

HIGHER SCORES INDICATE HIGHER LEVELS OF WELLNESS

SCORE

WILD ⁵☆ Wellness®
Wellness Interventions for Life's Demands

© Copyright 2019 Saundra Jain & Rakesh Jain. All Rights Reserved.

PHASE 2 REFLECTIONS

Congratulations! You have successfully completed Phase 2 of LiveWell90. This is another opportunity to reflect on your practices during Phase 2, allowing you to make minor adjustments regarding any barriers you may have encountered. No matter what your experiences have been during Phase 2 - positive, negative or mixed - we strongly encourage you to take the time to complete this section. We believe you will uncover useful information that may improve the final 30 days of your LiveWell90 experience.

1. What did I learn about myself during Phase 2 of LiveWell90?

_____

_____

_____

_____

_____

2. What sacrifices have I made to meet the program expectations of LiveWell90?

_____

_____

_____

_____

_____

3. What barriers did I encounter?

_____

_____

_____

_____

_____

PLANS for PHASE 3

Now that you have reviewed Phase 2 of your LiveWell90 journey, take a moment to answer the questions below. The goal is to identify ways to elevate your LiveWell90 experience.

1. **What can I do to increase the chances that I will successfully complete LiveWell90?**

    _____
    _____
    _____
    _____

2. **To successfully meet the LiveWell90 program expectations, sacrifices are required. Which sacrifice has been the most challenging?**

    _____
    _____
    _____
    _____

3. **List 3-5 ways I can elevate my LiveWell90 experience?**

    _____
    _____
    _____
    _____
    _____
    _____

Words of Advice

Perfection is **NOT** the goal! Set your goals high and do your best every day. Be kind to yourself as you begin making these changes. Change is never easy. If you miss a day or two, shake it off, regroup, and begin again. Do not throw in the towel. Remember to track your wellness practices using the Participant Tracking Form (page 131).

Phase 3

SUSTAIN

- Program Expectations
- Participant Tracking Form
- Daily Journaling & HERO Exercises
- HERO Wellness Scale (Day 90)

WILD 5⭐ Wellness®
Wellness Interventions for Life's Demands

Phase 3
SUSTAIN

PROGRAM EXPECTATIONS

Exercise	Exercise 30 minutes <u>at least 3 days</u> per week for 30 days, aim for at least moderate intensity*
Mindfulness	Practice mindfulness for at least 10 minutes <u>at least 3 days</u> per week for 30 days
Sleep	Implement 4 or more of the 6 sleep hygiene practices <u>at least 3 days</u> per week for 30 days
Social Connectedness	Meet or call a minimum of two friends or family members <u>at least 3 days</u> per week for 30 days
Nutrition	Log your meals/snacks/beverages/alcohol <u>at least 3 days</u> per week for 30 days [Follow the MIND diet principles as closely as you can]

* *Consult your healthcare provider before starting any exercise program. If you're unable to reach 30 minutes of exercise per day or reach moderate intensity as you begin the program that is fine. Do whatever you're capable of doing. Base the amount of time you exercise and the intensity of your exercise on your physical capabilities.*

WILD 5★ Wellness™

Wellness Interventions for Life's Demands

LiveWell90

Participant Tracking Form

Phase 3: SUSTAIN

Start Date: _____

	Exercise Did I exercise today following the FID principles?		Mindfulness Did I mindfully meditate at least 10 minutes today?		Sleep Did I implement 4 or more of the 6 sleep hygiene practices?		Connectedness Did I socially connect with at least 2 people today?		Nutrition Did I log my meals, snacks, and beverages, including alcohol today?		HERO Did I complete my HERO exercises today?	
	YES	NO	YES	NO	YES	NO	YES	NO	YES	NO	YES	NO
1	○	○	○	○	○	○	○	○	○	○	○	○
2	○	○	○	○	○	○	○	○	○	○	○	○
3	○	○	○	○	○	○	○	○	○	○	○	○
4	○	○	○	○	○	○	○	○	○	○	○	○
5	○	○	○	○	○	○	○	○	○	○	○	○
6	○	○	○	○	○	○	○	○	○	○	○	○
7	○	○	○	○	○	○	○	○	○	○	○	○
8	○	○	○	○	○	○	○	○	○	○	○	○
9	○	○	○	○	○	○	○	○	○	○	○	○
10	○	○	○	○	○	○	○	○	○	○	○	○
11	○	○	○	○	○	○	○	○	○	○	○	○
12	○	○	○	○	○	○	○	○	○	○	○	○
13	○	○	○	○	○	○	○	○	○	○	○	○
14	○	○	○	○	○	○	○	○	○	○	○	○
15	○	○	○	○	○	○	○	○	○	○	○	○
	YES	NO	YES	NO	YES	NO	YES	NO	YES	NO	YES	NO

© Copyright 2019 Saundra Jain & Rakesh Jain. All Rights Reserved.

Day	Exercise Did I exercise today following the FID principles?		Mindfulness Did I mindfully meditate at least 10 minutes today?		Sleep Did I implement 4 or more of the 6 sleep hygiene practices?		Connectedness Did I socially connect with at least 2 people today?		Nutrition Did I log my meals, snacks, and beverages, including alcohol today?		HERO Did I complete my HERO exercises today?	
	YES	NO	YES	NO	YES	NO	YES	NO	YES	NO	YES	NO
16	○	○	○	○	○	○	○	○	○	○	○	○
17	○	○	○	○	○	○	○	○	○	○	○	○
18	○	○	○	○	○	○	○	○	○	○	○	○
19	○	○	○	○	○	○	○	○	○	○	○	○
20	○	○	○	○	○	○	○	○	○	○	○	○
21	○	○	○	○	○	○	○	○	○	○	○	○
22	○	○	○	○	○	○	○	○	○	○	○	○
23	○	○	○	○	○	○	○	○	○	○	○	○
24	○	○	○	○	○	○	○	○	○	○	○	○
25	○	○	○	○	○	○	○	○	○	○	○	○
26	○	○	○	○	○	○	○	○	○	○	○	○
27	○	○	○	○	○	○	○	○	○	○	○	○
28	○	○	○	○	○	○	○	○	○	○	○	○
29	○	○	○	○	○	○	○	○	○	○	○	○
30	○	○	○	○	○	○	○	○	○	○	○	○
	YES	NO	YES	NO	YES	NO	YES	NO	YES	NO	YES	NO

© Copyright 2019 Saundra Jain & Rakesh Jain. All Rights Reserved.

Daily Journaling and HERO Exercises

Using the *Daily Journaling Form* allows you to capture useful information on a daily basis about your LiveWell90 wellness practices. It asks you to document what you did each day to meet the program expectations for each of the 5 wellness components. You are also asked to record any barriers you encountered, and the solutions you used to overcome them.

HERO exercises are designed to improve your mental wellness. Doing them daily increases and enriches your levels of happiness, enthusiasm, resilience, and optimism.

Daily Journaling Form

EXERCISE	Exercise 30 minutes <u>at least 3 days</u> per week for 30 days, aim for at least moderate intensity
Type of Exercise	**Duration** _____ minutes
Intensity	☐ Low ☐ Moderate ☐ High

MINDFULNESS	Practice mindfulness at least 10 minutes <u>at least 3 days</u> per week for 30 days
Today's Guided Meditation(s)	

SLEEP	Implement 4 or more of the 6 sleep hygiene practices <u>at least 3 days</u> per week for 30 days
Implemented These Sleep Hygiene Practices	☐ No electronics 90 min before bed ☐ Sleep mask or blackout shades ☐ Regular bedtime ☐ No napping ☐ Warm bath/shower prior to bed ☐ Avoid caffeine 10 hrs before bed

SOCIAL CONNECTEDNESS	Meet or call at least two friends or family members <u>at least 3 days</u> per week for 30 days
Today's Social Contacts	**Friends** ☐ Call ☐ In-person **Family** ☐ Call ☐ In-person

NUTRITION	Log your daily meals/snacks/beverages/ alcohol <u>at least 3 days</u> per week for 30 days
Logged Meals/Snacks/Beverages/Alcohol	☐ Yes ☐ No
Strongly Recommended	
Implemented MIND Diet Principles	☐ Yes ☐ No
Practiced Mindful Meal Meditation	☐ Breakfast ☐ Lunch ☐ Dinner

TODAY'S PROGRESS	
My Barrier(s)	
My Solution(s)	

HERO Exercises
*H*appiness • *E*nthusiasm • *R*esilience • *O*ptimism

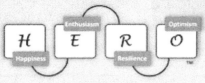

HAPPINESS & ENTHUSIASM ARE KNOWN TO LESSEN PAIN

---

1. Random acts of kindness will increase your happiness! Take a moment and write down two random acts of kindness you will put into action today. If you don't have time to execute your plan today, be sure to make it happen first thing tomorrow morning.

   a. _____

   _____

   b. _____

   _____

---

2. When it comes to outlook, do you fall on the positive or the negative side of the fence? Having a positive attitude about life improves enthusiasm. To increase your enthusiasm, mindfully consider your day and write down two examples of your positive attitude and/or actions.

   a. _____

   _____

   b. _____

   _____

Please take time to review your previous HERO exercises. Research shows that reflecting on past thoughts about wellness further strengthens and solidifies your HERO wellness traits. The HERO exercises are intentionally repeated every 8 days because repetition is crucial to learning and incorporating new ideas.

Let the winds of enthusiasm sweep through you. Live today with gusto.
~ Dale Carnegie

Daily Journaling Form

EXERCISE	Exercise 30 minutes <u>at least 3 days</u> per week for 30 days, aim for at least moderate intensity	
Type of Exercise		Duration	_____ minutes
Intensity	☐ Low	☐ Moderate	☐ High

MINDFULNESS	Practice mindfulness at least 10 minutes <u>at least 3 days</u> per week for 30 days
Today's Guided Meditation(s)	

SLEEP	Implement 4 or more of the 6 sleep hygiene practices <u>at least 3 days</u> per week for 30 days		
Implemented These Sleep Hygiene Practices	☐ No electronics 90 min before bed	☐ Sleep mask or blackout shades	☐ Regular bedtime
	☐ No napping	☐ Warm bath/shower prior to bed	☐ Avoid caffeine 10 hrs before bed

SOCIAL CONNECTEDNESS	Meet or call at least two friends or family members <u>at least 3 days</u> per week for 30 days	
	Friends	Family
Today's Social Contacts	☐ Call ☐ In-person	☐ Call ☐ In-person

NUTRITION	Log your daily meals/snacks/beverages/ alcohol <u>at least 3 days</u> per week for 30 days	
Logged Meals/Snacks/Beverages/Alcohol	☐ Yes	☐ No
Strongly Recommended		
Implemented MIND Diet Principles	☐ Yes	☐ No
Practiced Mindful Meal Meditation	☐ Breakfast ☐ Lunch	☐ Dinner

TODAY'S PROGRESS	
My Barrier(s)	
My Solution(s)	

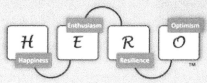

HERO Exercises
Happiness • Enthusiasm • Resilience • Optimism

RESILIENCE & OPTIMISM FERTILIZE A POSITIVE ATTITUDE

1. Being of service to others is a great way to build resilience. List two things you did today (or will do tomorrow) to give back to others or to brighten their day.

   a. _____

   _____

   b. _____

   _____

2. Is your glass half-full or half-empty? How you view the world matters! Write down two things that happened today that you viewed as negative. Take a moment and give this some thought, and then write down a less negative, or even a positive interpretation of the same events.

   a. _____

   _____

   b. _____

   _____

Please take time to review your previous HERO exercises. Research shows that reflecting on past thoughts about wellness further strengthens and solidifies your HERO wellness traits. The HERO exercises are intentionally repeated every 8 days because repetition is crucial to learning and incorporating new ideas.

Don't cry because it's over, smile because it happened.
~ Dr. Seuss

Daily Journaling Form

EXERCISE	Exercise 30 minutes at least 3 days per week for 30 days, aim for at least moderate intensity		
Type of Exercise		Duration	_____ minutes
Intensity	☐ Low	☐ Moderate	☐ High

MINDFULNESS	Practice mindfulness at least 10 minutes at least 3 days per week for 30 days
Today's Guided Meditation(s)	

SLEEP	Implement 4 or more of the 6 sleep hygiene practices at least 3 days per week for 30 days		
Implemented These Sleep Hygiene Practices	☐ No electronics 90 min before bed	☐ Sleep mask or blackout shades	☐ Regular bedtime
	☐ No napping	☐ Warm bath/shower prior to bed	☐ Avoid caffeine 10 hrs before bed

SOCIAL CONNECTEDNESS	Meet or call at least two friends or family members at least 3 days per week for 30 days	
	Friends	Family
Today's Social Contacts	☐ Call ☐ In-person	☐ Call ☐ In-person

NUTRITION	Log your daily meals/snacks/beverages/ alcohol at least 3 days per week for 30 days	
Logged Meals/Snacks/Beverages/Alcohol	☐ Yes	☐ No
Strongly Recommended		
Implemented MIND Diet Principles	☐ Yes	☐ No
Practiced Mindful Meal Meditation	☐ Breakfast ☐ Lunch ☐ Dinner	

TODAY'S PROGRESS	
My Barrier(s)	
My Solution(s)	

HERO Exercises
Happiness • Enthusiasm • Resilience • Optimism

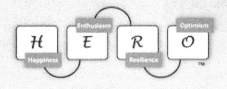

HAPPINESS & ENTHUSIASM PREDICT LOWER HEART RATE & BLOOD PRESSURE

---

1. Thinking about happy memories can positively impact your level of happiness! Write down two memories that bring a smile to your face. Next, spend a few minutes reliving each of these happy memories, and watch your current level of happiness increase.

   a. _____

   _____

   b. _____

   _____

2. Gratitude is known to increase feelings of happiness and enthusiasm. To increase these feelings, mindfully consider your day and write down two examples of things that happened today that increased your feelings of gratitude.

   a. _____

   _____

   b. _____

   _____

Please take time to review your previous HERO exercises. Research shows that reflecting on past thoughts about wellness further strengthens and solidifies your HERO wellness traits. The HERO exercises are intentionally repeated every 8 days because repetition is crucial to learning and incorporating new ideas.

There is nothing more contagious than exuberant enthusiasm.
~ Harry Houdini

Daily Journaling Form

EXERCISE	Exercise 30 minutes at least 3 days per week for 30 days, aim for at least moderate intensity		
Type of Exercise		Duration	_____ minutes
Intensity	☐ Low	☐ Moderate	☐ High

MINDFULNESS	Practice mindfulness at least 10 minutes at least 3 days per week for 30 days
Today's Guided Meditation(s)	

SLEEP	Implement 4 or more of the 6 sleep hygiene practices at least 3 days per week for 30 days		
Implemented These Sleep Hygiene Practices	☐ No electronics 90 min before bed	☐ Sleep mask or blackout shades	☐ Regular bedtime
	☐ No napping	☐ Warm bath/shower prior to bed	☐ Avoid caffeine 10 hrs before bed

SOCIAL CONNECTEDNESS	Meet or call at least two friends or family members at least 3 days per week for 30 days			
	Friends		Family	
Today's Social Contacts	☐ Call	☐ In-person	☐ Call	☐ In-person

NUTRITION	Log your daily meals/snacks/beverages/ alcohol at least 3 days per week for 30 days	
Logged Meals/Snacks/Beverages/Alcohol	☐ Yes	☐ No
Strongly Recommended		
Implemented MIND Diet Principles	☐ Yes	☐ No
Practiced Mindful Meal Meditation	☐ Breakfast ☐ Lunch	☐ Dinner

TODAY'S PROGRESS	
My Barrier(s)	
My Solution(s)	

HERO Exercises
Happiness • Enthusiasm • Resilience • Optimism

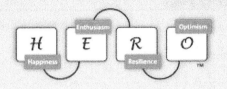

RESILIENCE & OPTIMISM ARE LINKED TO GREATER LIFE SATISFACTION

1. People are quick to point out faults and weaknesses. Acknowledging others' successes is a great way to build and strengthen your resilience while making another person feel great. Think of two people that have recently achieved some type of success, personal or work-related, and write down how you plan to acknowledge their achievement.

   a. _____

   _____

   b. _____

   _____

2. Have you heard of *Paying it Forward*? Someone does something kind for you and you pass it forward by doing something kind for another. Write down two times others have done something kind for you and how that made you feel. Make a plan to pass along those acts of kindness and brighten someone else's day.

   a. _____

   _____

   b. _____

   _____

Please take time to review your previous HERO exercises. Research shows that reflecting on past thoughts about wellness further strengthens and solidifies your HERO wellness traits. The HERO exercises are intentionally repeated every 8 days because repetition is crucial to learning and incorporating new ideas.

Even the darkest night will end and the sun will rise.
~ *J.R.R. Tolkien*

Daily Journaling Form

EXERCISE	Exercise 30 minutes at least 3 days per week for 30 days, aim for at least moderate intensity

Type of Exercise		Duration	_____ minutes
Intensity	☐ Low	☐ Moderate	☐ High

MINDFULNESS	Practice mindfulness at least 10 minutes at least 3 days per week for 30 days
Today's Guided Meditation(s)	

SLEEP	Implement 4 or more of the 6 sleep hygiene practices at least 3 days per week for 30 days

Implemented These Sleep Hygiene Practices	☐ No electronics 90 min before bed	☐ Sleep mask or blackout shades	☐ Regular bedtime
	☐ No napping	☐ Warm bath/shower prior to bed	☐ Avoid caffeine 10 hrs before bed

SOCIAL CONNECTEDNESS	Meet or call at least two friends or family members at least 3 days per week for 30 days

	Friends		Family	
Today's Social Contacts	☐ Call	☐ In-person	☐ Call	☐ In-person

NUTRITION	Log your daily meals/snacks/beverages/ alcohol at least 3 days per week for 30 days

Logged Meals/Snacks/Beverages/Alcohol	☐ Yes	☐ No
Strongly Recommended		
Implemented MIND Diet Principles	☐ Yes	☐ No
Practiced Mindful Meal Meditation	☐ Breakfast ☐ Lunch ☐ Dinner	

TODAY'S PROGRESS	
My Barrier(s)	
My Solution(s)	

HERO Exercises
*H*appiness • *E*nthusiasm • *R*esilience • *O*ptimism

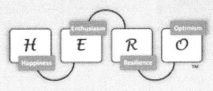

HAPPINESS & ENTHUSIASM ARE LINKED TO LONGEVITY

1. To increase your happiness, let's work on strengthening your happiness muscle. Take a moment and write down two positive things that you'd like to experience today. Also, two to three times today, find a few minutes to visualize and relish these positive experiences.

   a. _____

   _____

   b. _____

   _____

2. Having a goal or a project that inspires you will increase your enthusiasm. Write down two projects you find inspiring and set a start date. Put the date on your calendar with reminder alerts – make it happen and watch your enthusiasm improve!

   a. _____

   _____

   b. _____

   _____

Please take time to review your previous HERO exercises. Research shows that reflecting on past thoughts about wellness further strengthens and solidifies your HERO wellness traits. The HERO exercises are intentionally repeated every 8 days because repetition is crucial to learning and incorporating new ideas.

I am in charge of how I feel and today I am choosing happiness.
~ Anonymous

Daily Journaling Form

EXERCISE	Exercise 30 minutes at least 3 days per week for 30 days, aim for at least moderate intensity	
Type of Exercise		Duration _____ minutes
Intensity	☐ Low ☐ Moderate ☐ High	

MINDFULNESS	Practice mindfulness at least 10 minutes at least 3 days per week for 30 days
Today's Guided Meditation(s)	

SLEEP	Implement 4 or more of the 6 sleep hygiene practices at least 3 days per week for 30 days		
Implemented These Sleep Hygiene Practices	☐ No electronics 90 min before bed	☐ Sleep mask or blackout shades	☐ Regular bedtime
	☐ No napping	☐ Warm bath/shower prior to bed	☐ Avoid caffeine 10 hrs before bed

SOCIAL CONNECTEDNESS	Meet or call at least two friends or family members at least 3 days per week for 30 days	
Today's Social Contacts	Friends: ☐ Call ☐ In-person	Family: ☐ Call ☐ In-person

NUTRITION	Log your daily meals/snacks/beverages/alcohol at least 3 days per week for 30 days	
Logged Meals/Snacks/Beverages/Alcohol	☐ Yes	☐ No
Strongly Recommended		
Implemented MIND Diet Principles	☐ Yes	☐ No
Practiced Mindful Meal Meditation	☐ Breakfast ☐ Lunch ☐ Dinner	

TODAY'S PROGRESS	
My Barrier(s)	
My Solution(s)	

HERO Exercises
*H*appiness • *E*nthusiasm • *R*esilience • *O*ptimism

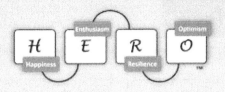

RESILIENT OPTIMISTS HAVE BETTER PHYSICAL HEALTH & BETTER RELATIONSHIPS

1. Resilience means the ability to bounce back from adversities. Write down 2 things about yourself that make you tough, and two skills you have used previously to overcome adversities. Remind yourself throughout the day that you genuinely possess these resilient traits.

    a. _____

    _____

    b. _____

    _____

2. Optimism often requires making a choice about how you view the world. Write down two positive things you want to happen tomorrow, and then spend a few minutes planning on how to make these optimistic attitudes/events a reality.

    a. _____

    _____

    b. _____

    _____

Please take time to review your previous HERO exercises. Research shows that reflecting on past thoughts about wellness further strengthens and solidifies your HERO wellness traits. The HERO exercises are intentionally repeated every 8 days because repetition is crucial to learning and incorporating new ideas.

Write it on your heart that every day is the best day in the year.
~ *Ralph Waldo Emerson*

Daily Journaling Form

EXERCISE	Exercise 30 minutes at least 3 days per week for 30 days, aim for at least moderate intensity	
Type of Exercise		Duration _____ minutes
Intensity	☐ Low	☐ Moderate ☐ High

MINDFULNESS	Practice mindfulness at least 10 minutes at least 3 days per week for 30 days
Today's Guided Meditation(s)	

SLEEP	Implement 4 or more of the 6 sleep hygiene practices at least 3 days per week for 30 days		
Implemented These Sleep Hygiene Practices	☐ No electronics 90 min before bed	☐ Sleep mask or blackout shades	☐ Regular bedtime
	☐ No napping	☐ Warm bath/shower prior to bed	☐ Avoid caffeine 10 hrs before bed

SOCIAL CONNECTEDNESS	Meet or call at least two friends or family members at least 3 days per week for 30 days	
	Friends	**Family**
Today's Social Contacts	☐ Call ☐ In-person	☐ Call ☐ In-person

NUTRITION	Log your daily meals/snacks/beverages/ alcohol at least 3 days per week for 30 days	
Logged Meals/Snacks/Beverages/Alcohol	☐ Yes	☐ No
Strongly Recommended		
Implemented MIND Diet Principles	☐ Yes	☐ No
Practiced Mindful Meal Meditation	☐ Breakfast ☐ Lunch ☐ Dinner	

TODAY'S PROGRESS	
My Barrier(s)	
My Solution(s)	

HERO Exercises
Happiness • Enthusiasm • Resilience • Optimism

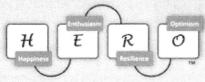

HAPPINESS & ENTHUSIASM ARE LINKED TO A STRONGER IMMUNE SYSTEM

---

1. In today's busy world, it's easy to overlook things that make us happy. Fast-paced lifestyles often become a barrier. Take a moment and mindfully reflect on your day, and write down two things that brought you happiness.

   a. _____

   _____

   b. _____

   _____

---

2. "Birds of a feather flock together," so surround yourself with happy and enthusiastic people. Write down the names of two people in your life that are happy and enthusiastic. Now, write down how and when you will connect with them.

   a. _____

   _____

   b. _____

   _____

Please take time to review your previous HERO exercises. Research shows that reflecting on past thoughts about wellness further strengthens and solidifies your HERO wellness traits. The HERO exercises are intentionally repeated every 8 days because repetition is crucial to learning and incorporating new ideas.

If you think sunshine brings you happiness, then you haven't danced in the rain.
~ *J.D. Salinger*

Daily Journaling Form

EXERCISE	Exercise 30 minutes <u>at least 3 days</u> per week for 30 days, aim for at least moderate intensity		
Type of Exercise		Duration	_____ minutes
Intensity	☐ Low	☐ Moderate	☐ High

MINDFULNESS	Practice mindfulness at least 10 minutes <u>at least 3 days</u> per week for 30 days
Today's Guided Meditation(s)	

SLEEP	Implement 4 or more of the 6 sleep hygiene practices <u>at least 3 days</u> per week for 30 days		
Implemented These Sleep Hygiene Practices	☐ No electronics 90 min before bed	☐ Sleep mask or blackout shades	☐ Regular bedtime
	☐ No napping	☐ Warm bath/shower prior to bed	☐ Avoid caffeine 10 hrs before bed

SOCIAL CONNECTEDNESS	Meet or call at least two friends or family members <u>at least 3 days</u> per week for 30 days	
	Friends	**Family**
Today's Social Contacts	☐ Call ☐ In-person	☐ Call ☐ In-person

NUTRITION	Log your daily meals/snacks/beverages/ alcohol <u>at least 3 days</u> per week for 30 days
Logged Meals/Snacks/Beverages/Alcohol	☐ Yes ☐ No
Strongly Recommended	
Implemented MIND Diet Principles	☐ Yes ☐ No
Practiced Mindful Meal Meditation	☐ Breakfast ☐ Lunch ☐ Dinner

TODAY'S PROGRESS	
My Barrier(s)	
My Solution(s)	

HERO Exercises
Happiness • Enthusiasm • Resilience • Optimism

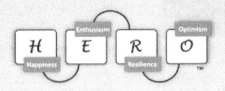

RESILIENT & OPTIMISTIC PEOPLE REPORT BETTER MENTAL HEALTH & LIVE LONGER

1. Dealing with life's challenges with humor builds resilience – the ability to bounce back from life's adversities. Write down two things that happened recently that you found humorous – things that made you smile or laugh.

    a. _____

    _____

    b. _____

    _____

2. Positive affirmations are a great way to build an optimistic mindset. Take a moment and write down two positive statements about yourself, your life, or your future. Purposefully remind yourself of these affirmations several times throughout your day.

    a. _____

    _____

    b. _____

    _____

Please take time to review your previous HERO exercises. Research shows that reflecting on past thoughts about wellness further strengthens and solidifies your HERO wellness traits. The HERO exercises are intentionally repeated every 8 days because repetition is crucial to learning and incorporating new ideas.

Resilience is the key. Discipline is a must.
~ *Anonymous*

Daily Journaling Form

EXERCISE	Exercise 30 minutes at least 3 days per week for 30 days, aim for at least moderate intensity

Type of Exercise		Duration	_____ minutes
Intensity	☐ Low	☐ Moderate	☐ High

MINDFULNESS	Practice mindfulness at least 10 minutes at least 3 days per week for 30 days

Today's Guided Meditation(s)	

SLEEP	Implement 4 or more of the 6 sleep hygiene practices at least 3 days per week for 30 days

Implemented These Sleep Hygiene Practices	☐ No electronics 90 min before bed	☐ Sleep mask or blackout shades	☐ Regular bedtime
	☐ No napping	☐ Warm bath/shower prior to bed	☐ Avoid caffeine 10 hrs before bed

SOCIAL CONNECTEDNESS	Meet or call at least two friends or family members at least 3 days per week for 30 days

Today's Social Contacts	**Friends** ☐ Call ☐ In-person	**Family** ☐ Call ☐ In-person

NUTRITION	Log your daily meals/snacks/beverages/ alcohol at least 3 days per week for 30 days

Logged Meals/Snacks/Beverages/Alcohol	☐ Yes ☐ No
Strongly Recommended	
Implemented MIND Diet Principles	☐ Yes ☐ No
Practiced Mindful Meal Meditation	☐ Breakfast ☐ Lunch ☐ Dinner

TODAY'S PROGRESS	
My Barrier(s)	
My Solution(s)	

HERO Exercises
Happiness • Enthusiasm • Resilience • Optimism

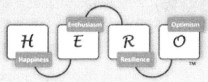

HAPPINESS & ENTHUSIASM ARE KNOWN TO LESSEN PAIN

1. Random acts of kindness will increase your happiness! Take a moment and write down two random acts of kindness you will put into action today. If you don't have time to execute your plan today, be sure to make it happen first thing tomorrow morning.

    a. _____

    _____

    b. _____

    _____

2. When it comes to outlook, do you fall on the positive or the negative side of the fence? Having a positive attitude about life improves enthusiasm. To increase your enthusiasm, mindfully consider your day and write down two examples of your positive attitude and/or actions.

    a. _____

    _____

    b. _____

    _____

Please take time to review your previous HERO exercises. Research shows that reflecting on past thoughts about wellness further strengthens and solidifies your HERO wellness traits. The HERO exercises are intentionally repeated every 8 days because repetition is crucial to learning and incorporating new ideas.

Happiness is only real when shared.
~ *Christopher McCandless*

Daily Journaling Form

EXERCISE	Exercise 30 minutes <u>at least 3 days</u> per week for 30 days, aim for at least moderate intensity

Type of Exercise		Duration	_____ minutes
Intensity	☐ Low	☐ Moderate	☐ High

MINDFULNESS	Practice mindfulness at least 10 minutes <u>at least 3 days</u> per week for 30 days
Today's Guided Meditation(s)	

SLEEP	Implement 4 or more of the 6 sleep hygiene practices <u>at least 3 days</u> per week for 30 days

Implemented These Sleep Hygiene Practices	☐ No electronics 90 min before bed	☐ Sleep mask or blackout shades	☐ Regular bedtime
	☐ No napping	☐ Warm bath/shower prior to bed	☐ Avoid caffeine 10 hrs before bed

SOCIAL CONNECTEDNESS	Meet or call at least two friends or family members <u>at least 3 days</u> per week for 30 days

Today's Social Contacts	Friends		Family	
	☐ Call	☐ In-person	☐ Call	☐ In-person

NUTRITION	Log your daily meals/snacks/beverages/ alcohol <u>at least 3 days</u> per week for 30 days
Logged Meals/Snacks/Beverages/Alcohol	☐ Yes ☐ No

Strongly Recommended	
Implemented MIND Diet Principles	☐ Yes ☐ No
Practiced Mindful Meal Meditation	☐ Breakfast ☐ Lunch ☐ Dinner

TODAY'S PROGRESS	
My Barrier(s)	
My Solution(s)	

HERO Exercises
Happiness • Enthusiasm • Resilience • Optimism

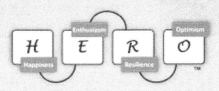

RESILIENCE & OPTIMISM FERTILIZE A POSITIVE ATTITUDE

---

1. Being of service to others is a great way to build resilience. List two things you did today (or will do tomorrow) to give back to others or to brighten their day.

   a. _____

   _____

   b. _____

   _____

---

2. Is your glass half-full or half-empty? How you view the world matters! Write down two things that happened today that you viewed as negative. Take a moment and give this some thought, and then write down a less negative, or even a positive interpretation of the same events.

   a. _____

   _____

   b. _____

   _____

Please take time to review your previous HERO exercises. Research shows that reflecting on past thoughts about wellness further strengthens and solidifies your HERO wellness traits. The HERO exercises are intentionally repeated every 8 days because repetition is crucial to learning and incorporating new ideas.

"Instead of worrying about what you cannot control,
shift your energy to what you can create."

~ Roy T. Bennett

Daily Journaling Form

EXERCISE	Exercise 30 minutes at least 3 days per week for 30 days, aim for at least moderate intensity

Type of Exercise		Duration	_____ minutes
Intensity	☐ Low	☐ Moderate	☐ High

MINDFULNESS	Practice mindfulness at least 10 minutes at least 3 days per week for 30 days

Today's Guided Meditation(s)	

SLEEP	Implement 4 or more of the 6 sleep hygiene practices at least 3 days per week for 30 days

Implemented These Sleep Hygiene Practices	☐ No electronics 90 min before bed	☐ Sleep mask or blackout shades	☐ Regular bedtime
	☐ No napping	☐ Warm bath/shower prior to bed	☐ Avoid caffeine 10 hrs before bed

SOCIAL CONNECTEDNESS	Meet or call at least two friends or family members at least 3 days per week for 30 days

	Friends		Family	
Today's Social Contacts	☐ Call	☐ In-person	☐ Call	☐ In-person

NUTRITION	Log your daily meals/snacks/beverages/ alcohol at least 3 days per week for 30 days

Logged Meals/Snacks/Beverages/Alcohol	☐ Yes	☐ No
Strongly Recommended		
Implemented MIND Diet Principles	☐ Yes	☐ No
Practiced Mindful Meal Meditation	☐ Breakfast ☐ Lunch ☐ Dinner	

TODAY'S PROGRESS	
My Barrier(s)	
My Solution(s)	

HERO Exercises
*H*appiness • *E*nthusiasm • *R*esilience • *O*ptimism

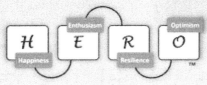

> **HAPPINESS & ENTHUSIASM PREDICT LOWER HEART RATE & BLOOD PRESSURE**

1. Thinking about happy memories can positively impact your level of happiness! Write down two memories that bring a smile to your face. Next, spend a few minutes reliving each of these happy memories, and watch your current level of happiness increase.

    a. _____

    _____

    b. _____

    _____

2. Gratitude is known to increase feelings of happiness and enthusiasm. To increase these feelings, mindfully consider your day and write down two examples of things that happened today that increased your feelings of gratitude.

    a. _____

    _____

    b. _____

    _____

Please take time to review your previous HERO exercises. Research shows that reflecting on past thoughts about wellness further strengthens and solidifies your HERO wellness traits. The HERO exercises are intentionally repeated every 8 days because repetition is crucial to learning and incorporating new ideas.

Happiness is a conscious choice, not an automatic response.
~ Mildred Barthel

Daily Journaling Form

EXERCISE	Exercise 30 minutes <u>at least 3 days</u> per week for 30 days, aim for at least moderate intensity		
Type of Exercise		**Duration**	_____ minutes
Intensity	☐ Low	☐ Moderate	☐ High

MINDFULNESS	Practice mindfulness at least 10 minutes <u>at least 3 days</u> per week for 30 days
Today's Guided Meditation(s)	

SLEEP	Implement 4 or more of the 6 sleep hygiene practices <u>at least 3 days</u> per week for 30 days	
Implemented These Sleep Hygiene Practices	☐ No electronics 90 min before bed	☐ Sleep mask or blackout shades ☐ Regular bedtime
	☐ No napping	☐ Warm bath/shower prior to bed ☐ Avoid caffeine 10 hrs before bed

SOCIAL CONNECTEDNESS	Meet or call at least two friends or family members <u>at least 3 days</u> per week for 30 days	
Today's Social Contacts	**Friends** ☐ Call ☐ In-person	**Family** ☐ Call ☐ In-person

NUTRITION	Log your daily meals/snacks/beverages/ alcohol <u>at least 3 days</u> per week for 30 days	
Logged Meals/Snacks/Beverages/Alcohol	☐ Yes	☐ No
Strongly Recommended		
Implemented MIND Diet Principles	☐ Yes	☐ No
Practiced Mindful Meal Meditation	☐ Breakfast ☐ Lunch ☐ Dinner	

TODAY'S PROGRESS	
My Barrier(s)	
My Solution(s)	

HERO Exercises
*H*appiness • *E*nthusiasm • *R*esilience • *O*ptimism

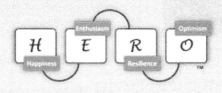

RESILIENCE & OPTIMISM ARE LINKED TO GREATER LIFE SATISFACTION

1. People are quick to point out faults and weaknesses. Acknowledging others' successes is a great way to build and strengthen your resilience while making another person feel great. Think of two people that have recently achieved some type of success, personal or work-related, and write down how you plan to acknowledge their achievement.

    a. _____

    _____

    b. _____

    _____

2. Have you heard of *Paying it Forward*? Someone does something kind for you and you pass it forward by doing something kind for another. Write down two times others have done something kind for you and how that made you feel. Make a plan to pass along those acts of kindness and brighten someone else's day.

    a. _____

    _____

    b. _____

    _____

Please take time to review your previous HERO exercises. Research shows that reflecting on past thoughts about wellness further strengthens and solidifies your HERO wellness traits. The HERO exercises are intentionally repeated every 8 days because repetition is crucial to learning and incorporating new ideas.

When I look at the future, it's so bright it burns my eyes!
~ Oprah Winfrey

Daily Journaling Form

EXERCISE	Exercise 30 minutes at least 3 days per week for 30 days, aim for at least moderate intensity

Type of Exercise		Duration	_____ minutes
Intensity	☐ Low	☐ Moderate	☐ High

MINDFULNESS	Practice mindfulness at least 10 minutes at least 3 days per week for 30 days

Today's Guided Meditation(s)	

SLEEP	Implement 4 or more of the 6 sleep hygiene practices at least 3 days per week for 30 days

Implemented These Sleep Hygiene Practices	☐ No electronics 90 min before bed	☐ Sleep mask or blackout shades	☐ Regular bedtime
	☐ No napping	☐ Warm bath/shower prior to bed	☐ Avoid caffeine 10 hrs before bed

SOCIAL CONNECTEDNESS	Meet or call at least two friends or family members at least 3 days per week for 30 days

Today's Social Contacts	Friends		Family	
	☐ Call	☐ In-person	☐ Call	☐ In-person

NUTRITION	Log your daily meals/snacks/beverages/alcohol at least 3 days per week for 30 days

Logged Meals/Snacks/Beverages/Alcohol	☐ Yes	☐ No

Strongly Recommended		
Implemented MIND Diet Principles	☐ Yes	☐ No
Practiced Mindful Meal Meditation	☐ Breakfast ☐ Lunch	☐ Dinner

TODAY'S PROGRESS	
My Barrier(s)	
My Solution(s)	

HERO Exercises
*H*appiness • *E*nthusiasm • *R*esilience • *O*ptimism

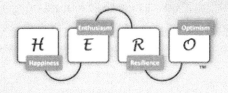

HAPPINESS & ENTHUSIASM ARE LINKED TO LONGEVITY

1. To increase your happiness, let's work on strengthening your happiness muscle. Take a moment and write down two positive things that you'd like to experience today. Also, two to three times today, find a few minutes to visualize and relish these positive experiences.

    a. _____

    _____

    b. _____

    _____

2. Having a goal or a project that inspires you will increase your enthusiasm. Write down two projects you find inspiring and set a start date. Put the date on your calendar with reminder alerts – make it happen and watch your enthusiasm improve!

    a. _____

    _____

    b. _____

    _____

Please take time to review your previous HERO exercises. Research shows that reflecting on past thoughts about wellness further strengthens and solidifies your HERO wellness traits. The HERO exercises are intentionally repeated every 8 days because repetition is crucial to learning and incorporating new ideas.

To fall in love with yourself is the first secret to happiness.
~ *Robert Morely*

Daily Journaling Form

EXERCISE	Exercise 30 minutes <u>at least 3 days</u> per week for 30 days, aim for at least moderate intensity

Type of Exercise		Duration	_____ minutes
Intensity	☐ Low	☐ Moderate	☐ High

MINDFULNESS	Practice mindfulness at least 10 minutes <u>at least 3 days</u> per week for 30 days

Today's Guided Meditation(s)	

SLEEP	Implement 4 or more of the 6 sleep hygiene practices <u>at least 3 days</u> per week for 30 days

Implemented These Sleep Hygiene Practices	☐ No electronics 90 min before bed	☐ Sleep mask or blackout shades	☐ Regular bedtime
	☐ No napping	☐ Warm bath/shower prior to bed	☐ Avoid caffeine 10 hrs before bed

SOCIAL CONNECTEDNESS	Meet or call at least two friends or family members <u>at least 3 days</u> per week for 30 days

	Friends		Family	
Today's Social Contacts	☐ Call	☐ In-person	☐ Call	☐ In-person

NUTRITION	Log your daily meals/snacks/beverages/ alcohol <u>at least 3 days</u> per week for 30 days

Logged Meals/Snacks/Beverages/Alcohol	☐ Yes	☐ No
Strongly Recommended		
Implemented MIND Diet Principles	☐ Yes	☐ No
Practiced Mindful Meal Meditation	☐ Breakfast ☐ Lunch ☐ Dinner	

TODAY'S PROGRESS	
My Barrier(s)	
My Solution(s)	

HERO Exercises
Happiness • Enthusiasm • Resilience • Optimism

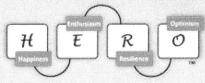

RESILIENT OPTIMISTS HAVE BETTER PHYSICAL HEALTH & BETTER RELATIONSHIPS

1. Resilience means the ability to bounce back from adversities. Write down 2 things about yourself that make you tough, and two skills you have used previously to overcome adversities. Remind yourself throughout the day that you genuinely possess these resilient traits.

    a. _____

    _____

    b. _____

    _____

2. Optimism often requires making a choice about how you view the world. Write down two positive things you want to happen tomorrow, and then spend a few minutes planning on how to make these optimistic attitudes/events a reality.

    a. _____

    _____

    b. _____

    _____

Please take time to review your previous HERO exercises. Research shows that reflecting on past thoughts about wellness further strengthens and solidifies your HERO wellness traits. The HERO exercises are intentionally repeated every 8 days because repetition is crucial to learning and incorporating new ideas.

It takes no more time to see the good side of life than to see the bad.
~ *Jimmy Buffett*

Daily Journaling Form

EXERCISE	Exercise 30 minutes at least 3 days per week for 30 days, aim for at least moderate intensity	
Type of Exercise	Duration	_____ minutes
Intensity	☐ Low ☐ Moderate ☐ High	

MINDFULNESS	Practice mindfulness at least 10 minutes at least 3 days per week for 30 days
Today's Guided Meditation(s)	

SLEEP	Implement 4 or more of the 6 sleep hygiene practices at least 3 days per week for 30 days		
Implemented These Sleep Hygiene Practices	☐ No electronics 90 min before bed	☐ Sleep mask or blackout shades	☐ Regular bedtime
	☐ No napping	☐ Warm bath/shower prior to bed	☐ Avoid caffeine 10 hrs before bed

SOCIAL CONNECTEDNESS	Meet or call at least two friends or family members at least 3 days per week for 30 days	
Today's Social Contacts	**Friends** ☐ Call ☐ In-person	**Family** ☐ Call ☐ In-person

NUTRITION	Log your daily meals/snacks/beverages/ alcohol at least 3 days per week for 30 days	
Logged Meals/Snacks/Beverages/Alcohol	☐ Yes	☐ No
Strongly Recommended		
Implemented MIND Diet Principles	☐ Yes	☐ No
Practiced Mindful Meal Meditation	☐ Breakfast ☐ Lunch ☐ Dinner	

TODAY'S PROGRESS	
My Barrier(s)	
My Solution(s)	

HERO Exercises
Happiness • Enthusiasm • Resilience • Optimism

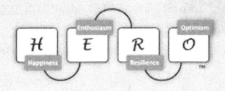

HAPPINESS & ENTHUSIASM ARE LINKED TO A STRONGER IMMUNE SYSTEM

1. In today's busy world, it's easy to overlook things that make us happy. Fast-paced lifestyles often become a barrier. Take a moment and mindfully reflect on your day, and write down two things that brought you happiness.

    a. _____

    _____

    b. _____

    _____

2. "Birds of a feather flock together," so surround yourself with happy and enthusiastic people. Write down the names of two people in your life that are happy and enthusiastic. Now, write down how and when you will connect with them.

    a. _____

    _____

    b. _____

    _____

Please take time to review your previous HERO exercises. Research shows that reflecting on past thoughts about wellness further strengthens and solidifies your HERO wellness traits. The HERO exercises are intentionally repeated every 8 days because repetition is crucial to learning and incorporating new ideas.

Growth itself contains the germ of happiness.
~ *Pearl S. Buck*

Daily Journaling Form

EXERCISE	Exercise 30 minutes <u>at least 3 days</u> per week for 30 days, aim for at least moderate intensity	
Type of Exercise		Duration _____ minutes
Intensity	☐ Low	☐ Moderate ☐ High

MINDFULNESS	Practice mindfulness at least 10 minutes <u>at least 3 days</u> per week for 30 days
Today's Guided Meditation(s)	

SLEEP	Implement 4 or more of the 6 sleep hygiene practices <u>at least 3 days</u> per week for 30 days		
Implemented These Sleep Hygiene Practices	☐ No electronics 90 min before bed	☐ Sleep mask or blackout shades	☐ Regular bedtime
	☐ No napping	☐ Warm bath/shower prior to bed	☐ Avoid caffeine 10 hrs before bed

SOCIAL CONNECTEDNESS	Meet or call at least two friends or family members <u>at least 3 days</u> per week for 30 days	
	Friends	Family
Today's Social Contacts	☐ Call ☐ In-person	☐ Call ☐ In-person

NUTRITION	Log your daily meals/snacks/beverages/ alcohol <u>at least 3 days</u> per week for 30 days	
Logged Meals/Snacks/Beverages/Alcohol	☐ Yes	☐ No
Strongly Recommended		
Implemented MIND Diet Principles	☐ Yes	☐ No
Practiced Mindful Meal Meditation	☐ Breakfast ☐ Lunch	☐ Dinner

TODAY'S PROGRESS	
My Barrier(s)	
My Solution(s)	

HERO Exercises
*H*appiness • *E*nthusiasm • *R*esilience • *O*ptimism

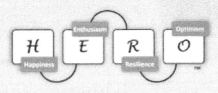

RESILIENT & OPTIMISTIC PEOPLE REPORT BETTER MENTAL HEALTH & LIVE LONGER

1. Dealing with life's challenges with humor builds resilience – the ability to bounce back from life's adversities. Write down two things that happened recently that you found humorous – things that made you smile or laugh.

   a. _____

   _____

   b. _____

   _____

2. Positive affirmations are a great way to build an optimistic mindset. Take a moment and write down two positive statements about yourself, your life, or your future. Purposefully remind yourself of these affirmations several times throughout your day.

   a. _____

   _____

   b. _____

   _____

Please take time to review your previous HERO exercises. Research shows that reflecting on past thoughts about wellness further strengthens and solidifies your HERO wellness traits. The HERO exercises are intentionally repeated every 8 days because repetition is crucial to learning and incorporating new ideas.

If all you can do is crawl, start crawling.
~ Rumi

Daily Journaling Form

EXERCISE	Exercise 30 minutes <u>at least 3 days</u> per week for 30 days, aim for at least moderate intensity		
Type of Exercise		Duration	_____ minutes
Intensity	☐ Low	☐ Moderate	☐ High

MINDFULNESS	Practice mindfulness at least 10 minutes <u>at least 3 days</u> per week for 30 days
Today's Guided Meditation(s)	

SLEEP	Implement 4 or more of the 6 sleep hygiene practices <u>at least 3 days</u> per week for 30 days		
Implemented These Sleep Hygiene Practices	☐ No electronics 90 min before bed	☐ Sleep mask or blackout shades	☐ Regular bedtime
	☐ No napping	☐ Warm bath/shower prior to bed	☐ Avoid caffeine 10 hrs before bed

SOCIAL CONNECTEDNESS	Meet or call at least two friends or family members <u>at least 3 days</u> per week for 30 days			
	Friends		Family	
Today's Social Contacts	☐ Call	☐ In-person	☐ Call	☐ In-person

NUTRITION	Log your daily meals/snacks/beverages/ alcohol <u>at least 3 days</u> per week for 30 days	
Logged Meals/Snacks/Beverages/Alcohol	☐ Yes	☐ No
Strongly Recommended		
Implemented MIND Diet Principles	☐ Yes	☐ No
Practiced Mindful Meal Meditation	☐ Breakfast ☐ Lunch ☐ Dinner	

TODAY'S PROGRESS	
My Barrier(s)	
My Solution(s)	

HERO Exercises
*H*appiness • *E*nthusiasm • *R*esilience • *O*ptimism

HAPPINESS & ENTHUSIASM ARE KNOWN TO LESSEN PAIN

---

1. Random acts of kindness will increase your happiness! Take a moment and write down two random acts of kindness you will put into action today. If you don't have time to execute your plan today, be sure to make it happen first thing tomorrow morning.

   a. _____

   _____

   b. _____

   _____

2. When it comes to outlook, do you fall on the positive or the negative side of the fence? Having a positive attitude about life improves enthusiasm. To increase your enthusiasm, mindfully consider your day and write down two examples of your positive attitude and/or actions.

   a. _____

   _____

   b. _____

   _____

Please take time to review your previous HERO exercises. Research shows that reflecting on past thoughts about wellness further strengthens and solidifies your HERO wellness traits. The HERO exercises are intentionally repeated every 8 days because repetition is crucial to learning and incorporating new ideas.

Nothing great was ever achieved without enthusiasm.
~ *Ralph Waldo Emerson*

Daily Journaling Form

EXERCISE	Exercise 30 minutes <u>at least 3 days</u> per week for 30 days, aim for at least moderate intensity		
Type of Exercise		**Duration**	_____ minutes
Intensity	☐ Low	☐ Moderate	☐ High

MINDFULNESS	Practice mindfulness at least 10 minutes <u>at least 3 days</u> per week for 30 days
Today's Guided Meditation(s)	

SLEEP	Implement 4 or more of the 6 sleep hygiene practices <u>at least 3 days</u> per week for 30 days		
Implemented These Sleep Hygiene Practices	☐ No electronics 90 min before bed	☐ Sleep mask or blackout shades	☐ Regular bedtime
	☐ No napping	☐ Warm bath/shower prior to bed	☐ Avoid caffeine 10 hrs before bed

SOCIAL CONNECTEDNESS	Meet or call at least two friends or family members <u>at least 3 days</u> per week for 30 days	
Today's Social Contacts	**Friends** ☐ Call ☐ In-person	**Family** ☐ Call ☐ In-person

NUTRITION	Log your daily meals/snacks/beverages/ alcohol <u>at least 3 days</u> per week for 30 days	
Logged Meals/Snacks/Beverages/Alcohol	☐ Yes	☐ No
Strongly Recommended		
Implemented MIND Diet Principles	☐ Yes	☐ No
Practiced Mindful Meal Meditation	☐ Breakfast ☐ Lunch ☐ Dinner	

TODAY'S PROGRESS	
My Barrier(s)	
My Solution(s)	

HERO Exercises
Happiness • Enthusiasm • Resilience • Optimism

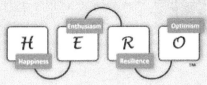

RESILIENCE & OPTIMISM FERTILIZE A POSITIVE ATTITUDE

1. Being of service to others is a great way to build resilience. List two things you did today
    (or will do tomorrow) to give back to others or to brighten their day.

    a. _____

        _____

    b. _____

        _____

2. Is your glass half-full or half-empty? How you view the world matters! Write down two
    things that happened today that you viewed as negative. Take a moment and give this
    some thought, and then write down a less negative, or even a positive interpretation of
    the same events.

    a. _____

        _____

    b. _____

        _____

**Please take time to review your previous HERO exercises. Research shows that
reflecting on past thoughts about wellness further strengthens and solidifies your
HERO wellness traits. The HERO exercises are intentionally repeated every 8 days
because repetition is crucial to learning and incorporating new ideas.**

You are never too old to set another goal or to dream a new dream.
~ *C.S. Lewis*

Daily Journaling Form

EXERCISE	Exercise 30 minutes at least 3 days per week for 30 days, aim for at least moderate intensity		
Type of Exercise		Duration	_____ minutes
Intensity	☐ Low	☐ Moderate	☐ High

MINDFULNESS	Practice mindfulness at least 10 minutes at least 3 days per week for 30 days
Today's Guided Meditation(s)	

SLEEP	Implement 4 or more of the 6 sleep hygiene practices at least 3 days per week for 30 days		
Implemented These Sleep Hygiene Practices	☐ No electronics 90 min before bed	☐ Sleep mask or blackout shades	☐ Regular bedtime
	☐ No napping	☐ Warm bath/shower prior to bed	☐ Avoid caffeine 10 hrs before bed

SOCIAL CONNECTEDNESS	Meet or call at least two friends or family members at least 3 days per week for 30 days			
	Friends		**Family**	
Today's Social Contacts	☐ Call	☐ In-person	☐ Call	☐ In-person

NUTRITION	Log your daily meals/snacks/beverages/ alcohol at least 3 days per week for 30 days		
Logged Meals/Snacks/Beverages/Alcohol	☐ Yes		☐ No
Strongly Recommended			
Implemented MIND Diet Principles	☐ Yes		☐ No
Practiced Mindful Meal Meditation	☐ Breakfast	☐ Lunch	☐ Dinner

TODAY'S PROGRESS	
My Barrier(s)	
My Solution(s)	

HERO Exercises
*H*appiness • *E*nthusiasm • *R*esilience • *O*ptimism

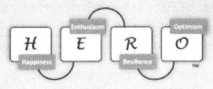

HAPPINESS & ENTHUSIASM PREDICT LOWER HEART RATE & BLOOD PRESSURE

1. Thinking about happy memories can positively impact your level of happiness! Write down two memories that bring a smile to your face. Next, spend a few minutes reliving each of these happy memories, and watch your current level of happiness increase.

   a. _____

   _____

   b. _____

   _____

2. Gratitude is known to increase feelings of happiness and enthusiasm. To increase these feelings, mindfully consider your day and write down two examples of things that happened today that increased your feelings of gratitude.

   a. _____

   _____

   b. _____

   _____

Please take time to review your previous HERO exercises. Research shows that reflecting on past thoughts about wellness further strengthens and solidifies your HERO wellness traits. The HERO exercises are intentionally repeated every 8 days because repetition is crucial to learning and incorporating new ideas.

Enthusiasm makes ordinary people extraordinary.
~ Anonymous

Daily Journaling Form

EXERCISE	Exercise 30 minutes <u>at least 3 days</u> per week for 30 days, aim for at least moderate intensity

Type of Exercise		Duration	_____ minutes
Intensity	☐ Low	☐ Moderate	☐ High

MINDFULNESS	Practice mindfulness at least 10 minutes <u>at least 3 days</u> per week for 30 days

Today's Guided Meditation(s)	

SLEEP	Implement 4 or more of the 6 sleep hygiene practices <u>at least 3 days</u> per week for 30 days

Implemented These Sleep Hygiene Practices	☐ No electronics 90 min before bed	☐ Sleep mask or blackout shades	☐ Regular bedtime
	☐ No napping	☐ Warm bath/shower prior to bed	☐ Avoid caffeine 10 hrs before bed

SOCIAL CONNECTEDNESS	Meet or call at least two friends or family members <u>at least 3 days</u> per week for 30 days

Today's Social Contacts	Friends		Family	
	☐ Call	☐ In-person	☐ Call	☐ In-person

NUTRITION	Log your daily meals/snacks/beverages/ alcohol <u>at least 3 days</u> per week for 30 days

Logged Meals/Snacks/Beverages/Alcohol	☐ Yes	☐ No
Strongly Recommended		
Implemented MIND Diet Principles	☐ Yes	☐ No
Practiced Mindful Meal Meditation	☐ Breakfast ☐ Lunch ☐ Dinner	

TODAY'S PROGRESS	
My Barrier(s)	
My Solution(s)	

HERO Exercises
Happiness • Enthusiasm • Resilience • Optimism

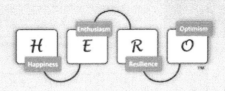

RESILIENCE & OPTIMISM ARE LINKED TO GREATER LIFE SATISFACTION

---

1. People are quick to point out faults and weaknesses. Acknowledging others' successes is a great way to build and strengthen your resilience while making another person feel great. Think of two people that have recently achieved some type of success, personal or work-related, and write down how you plan to acknowledge their achievement.

   a. _____

   _____

   b. _____

   _____

2. Have you heard of *Paying it Forward*? Someone does something kind for you and you pass it forward by doing something kind for another. Write down two times others have done something kind for you and how that made you feel. Make a plan to pass along those acts of kindness and brighten someone else's day.

   a. _____

   _____

   b. _____

   _____

Please take time to review your previous HERO exercises. Research shows that reflecting on past thoughts about wellness further strengthens and solidifies your HERO wellness traits. The HERO exercises are intentionally repeated every 8 days because repetition is crucial to learning and incorporating new ideas.

Optimism is wide-open in contrast to pessimism's closed heart.
~ *Kathleen A. Brehony*

Daily Journaling Form

EXERCISE	Exercise 30 minutes at least 3 days per week for 30 days, aim for at least moderate intensity		
Type of Exercise		Duration	_____ minutes
Intensity	☐ Low	☐ Moderate	☐ High

MINDFULNESS	Practice mindfulness at least 10 minutes at least 3 days per week for 30 days
Today's Guided Meditation(s)	

SLEEP	Implement 4 or more of the 6 sleep hygiene practices at least 3 days per week for 30 days		
Implemented These Sleep Hygiene Practices	☐ No electronics 90 min before bed	☐ Sleep mask or blackout shades	☐ Regular bedtime
	☐ No napping	☐ Warm bath/shower prior to bed	☐ Avoid caffeine 10 hrs before bed

SOCIAL CONNECTEDNESS	Meet or call at least two friends or family members at least 3 days per week for 30 days	
Today's Social Contacts	**Friends** ☐ Call ☐ In-person	**Family** ☐ Call ☐ In-person

NUTRITION	Log your daily meals/snacks/beverages/ alcohol at least 3 days per week for 30 days	
Logged Meals/Snacks/Beverages/Alcohol	☐ Yes	☐ No
Strongly Recommended		
Implemented MIND Diet Principles	☐ Yes	☐ No
Practiced Mindful Meal Meditation	☐ Breakfast ☐ Lunch	☐ Dinner

TODAY'S PROGRESS	
My Barrier(s)	
My Solution(s)	

246

HERO Exercises
*H*appiness • *E*nthusiasm • *R*esilience • *O*ptimism

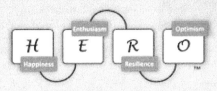

> ### HAPPINESS & ENTHUSIASM ARE LINKED TO LONGEVITY

1. To increase your happiness, let's work on strengthening your happiness muscle. Take a moment and write down two positive things that you'd like to experience today. Also, two to three times today, find a few minutes to visualize and relish these positive experiences.

   a. _____

   _____

   b. _____

   _____

2. Having a goal or a project that inspires you will increase your enthusiasm. Write down two projects you find inspiring and set a start date. Put the date on your calendar with reminder alerts – make it happen and watch your enthusiasm improve!

   a. _____

   _____

   b. _____

   _____

Please take time to review your previous HERO exercises. Research shows that reflecting on past thoughts about wellness further strengthens and solidifies your HERO wellness traits. The HERO exercises are intentionally repeated every 8 days because repetition is crucial to learning and incorporating new ideas.

Happiness depends upon ourselves.
~ *Aristotle*

Daily Journaling Form

EXERCISE	Exercise 30 minutes at least 3 days per week for 30 days, aim for at least moderate intensity	
Type of Exercise		Duration _____ minutes
Intensity	☐ Low	☐ Moderate ☐ High

MINDFULNESS	Practice mindfulness at least 10 minutes at least 3 days per week for 30 days
Today's Guided Meditation(s)	

SLEEP	Implement 4 or more of the 6 sleep hygiene practices at least 3 days per week for 30 days		
Implemented These Sleep Hygiene Practices	☐ No electronics 90 min before bed	☐ Sleep mask or blackout shades	☐ Regular bedtime
	☐ No napping	☐ Warm bath/shower prior to bed	☐ Avoid caffeine 10 hrs before bed

SOCIAL CONNECTEDNESS	Meet or call at least two friends or family members at least 3 days per week for 30 days	
	Friends	Family
Today's Social Contacts	☐ Call ☐ In-person	☐ Call ☐ In-person

NUTRITION	Log your daily meals/snacks/beverages/ alcohol at least 3 days per week for 30 days		
Logged Meals/Snacks/Beverages/Alcohol	☐ Yes	☐ No	
Strongly Recommended			
Implemented MIND Diet Principles	☐ Yes	☐ No	
Practiced Mindful Meal Meditation	☐ Breakfast	☐ Lunch	☐ Dinner

TODAY'S PROGRESS	
My Barrier(s)	
My Solution(s)	

HERO Exercises
*H*appiness • *E*nthusiasm • *R*esilience • *O*ptimism

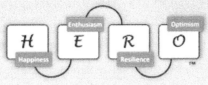

RESILIENT OPTIMISTS HAVE BETTER PHYSICAL HEALTH & BETTER RELATIONSHIPS

1. Resilience means the ability to bounce back from adversities. Write down 2 things about yourself that make you tough, and two skills you have used previously to overcome adversities. Remind yourself throughout the day that you genuinely possess these resilient traits.

    a. _____

    _____

    b. _____

    _____

2. Optimism often requires making a choice about how you view the world. Write down two positive things you want to happen tomorrow, and then spend a few minutes planning on how to make these optimistic attitudes/events a reality.

    a. _____

    _____

    b. _____

    _____

Please take time to review your previous HERO exercises. Research shows that reflecting on past thoughts about wellness further strengthens and solidifies your HERO wellness traits. The HERO exercises are intentionally repeated every 8 days because repetition is crucial to learning and incorporating new ideas.

He's a million rubber bands in his resilience.
~ *Alan K. Simpson*

Daily Journaling Form

EXERCISE	Exercise 30 minutes <u>at least 3 days</u> per week for 30 days, aim for at least moderate intensity	
Type of Exercise		Duration _____ minutes
Intensity	☐ Low	☐ Moderate ☐ High

MINDFULNESS	Practice mindfulness at least 10 minutes <u>at least 3 days</u> per week for 30 days
Today's Guided Meditation(s)	

SLEEP	Implement 4 or more of the 6 sleep hygiene practices <u>at least 3 days</u> per week for 30 days		
Implemented These Sleep Hygiene Practices	☐ No electronics 90 min before bed	☐ Sleep mask or blackout shades	☐ Regular bedtime
	☐ No napping	☐ Warm bath/shower prior to bed	☐ Avoid caffeine 10 hrs before bed

SOCIAL CONNECTEDNESS	Meet or call at least two friends or family members <u>at least 3 days</u> per week for 30 days	
	Friends	Family
Today's Social Contacts	☐ Call ☐ In-person	☐ Call ☐ In-person

NUTRITION	Log your daily meals/snacks/beverages/ alcohol <u>at least 3 days</u> per week for 30 days	
Logged Meals/Snacks/Beverages/Alcohol	☐ Yes	☐ No
Strongly Recommended		
Implemented MIND Diet Principles	☐ Yes	☐ No
Practiced Mindful Meal Meditation	☐ Breakfast ☐ Lunch ☐ Dinner	

TODAY'S PROGRESS	
My Barrier(s)	
My Solution(s)	

HERO Exercises
*H*appiness • *E*nthusiasm • *R*esilience • *O*ptimism

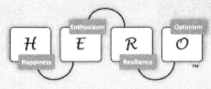

HAPPINESS & ENTHUSIASM ARE LINKED TO A STRONGER IMMUNE SYSTEM

1. In today's busy world, it's easy to overlook things that make us happy. Fast-paced lifestyles often become a barrier. Take a moment and mindfully reflect on your day, and write down two things that brought you happiness.

   a. _____

   _____

   b. _____

   _____

2. "Birds of a feather flock together," so surround yourself with happy and enthusiastic people. Write down the names of two people in your life that are happy and enthusiastic. Now, write down how and when you will connect with them.

   a. _____

   _____

   b. _____

   _____

Please take time to review your previous HERO exercises. Research shows that reflecting on past thoughts about wellness further strengthens and solidifies your HERO wellness traits. The HERO exercises are intentionally repeated every 8 days because repetition is crucial to learning and incorporating new ideas.

Creativity is a natural extension of our enthusiasm.
~ Earl Nightingale

Daily Journaling Form

EXERCISE	Exercise 30 minutes <u>at least 3 days</u> per week for 30 days, aim for at least moderate intensity		
Type of Exercise		Duration	_____ minutes
Intensity	☐ Low	☐ Moderate	☐ High

MINDFULNESS	Practice mindfulness at least 10 minutes <u>at least 3 days</u> per week for 30 days
Today's Guided Meditation(s)	

SLEEP	Implement 4 or more of the 6 sleep hygiene practices <u>at least 3 days</u> per week for 30 days		
Implemented These Sleep Hygiene Practices	☐ No electronics 90 min before bed	☐ Sleep mask or blackout shades	☐ Regular bedtime
	☐ No napping	☐ Warm bath/shower prior to bed	☐ Avoid caffeine 10 hrs before bed

SOCIAL CONNECTEDNESS	Meet or call at least two friends or family members <u>at least 3 days</u> per week for 30 days	
	Friends	Family
Today's Social Contacts	☐ Call ☐ In-person	☐ Call ☐ In-person

NUTRITION	Log your daily meals/snacks/beverages/ alcohol <u>at least 3 days</u> per week for 30 days	
Logged Meals/Snacks/Beverages/Alcohol	☐ Yes	☐ No
Strongly Recommended		
Implemented MIND Diet Principles	☐ Yes	☐ No
Practiced Mindful Meal Meditation	☐ Breakfast ☐ Lunch ☐ Dinner	

TODAY'S PROGRESS	
My Barrier(s)	
My Solution(s)	

HERO Exercises
*H*appiness • *E*nthusiasm • *R*esilience • *O*ptimism

RESILIENT & OPTIMISTIC PEOPLE REPORT BETTER MENTAL HEALTH & LIVE LONGER

1. Dealing with life's challenges with humor builds resilience – the ability to bounce back from life's adversities. Write down two things that happened recently that you found humorous – things that made you smile or laugh.

   a. _____

   _____

   b. _____

   _____

2. Positive affirmations are a great way to build an optimistic mindset. Take a moment and write down two positive statements about yourself, your life, or your future. Purposefully remind yourself of these affirmations several times throughout your day.

   a. _____

   _____

   b. _____

   _____

Please take time to review your previous HERO exercises. Research shows that reflecting on past thoughts about wellness further strengthens and solidifies your HERO wellness traits. The HERO exercises are intentionally repeated every 8 days because repetition is crucial to learning and incorporating new ideas.

Failure is a bruise not a tattoo.
~ Anonymous

Daily Journaling Form

EXERCISE	Exercise 30 minutes at least 3 days per week for 30 days, aim for at least moderate intensity

Type of Exercise		Duration	_____ minutes
Intensity	☐ Low	☐ Moderate	☐ High

MINDFULNESS	Practice mindfulness at least 10 minutes at least 3 days per week for 30 days
Today's Guided Meditation(s)	

SLEEP	Implement 4 or more of the 6 sleep hygiene practices at least 3 days per week for 30 days

Implemented These Sleep Hygiene Practices	☐ No electronics 90 min before bed	☐ Sleep mask or blackout shades	☐ Regular bedtime
	☐ No napping	☐ Warm bath/shower prior to bed	☐ Avoid caffeine 10 hrs before bed

SOCIAL CONNECTEDNESS	Meet or call at least two friends or family members at least 3 days per week for 30 days

Today's Social Contacts	Friends		Family	
	☐ Call	☐ In-person	☐ Call	☐ In-person

NUTRITION	Log your daily meals/snacks/beverages/ alcohol at least 3 days per week for 30 days

Logged Meals/Snacks/Beverages/Alcohol	☐ Yes	☐ No
Strongly Recommended		
Implemented MIND Diet Principles	☐ Yes	☐ No
Practiced Mindful Meal Meditation	☐ Breakfast ☐ Lunch ☐ Dinner	

TODAY'S PROGRESS	
My Barrier(s)	
My Solution(s)	

HERO Exercises
*H*appiness • *E*nthusiasm • *R*esilience • *O*ptimism

HAPPINESS & ENTHUSIASM ARE KNOWN TO LESSEN PAIN

1. Random acts of kindness will increase your happiness! Take a moment and write down two random acts of kindness you will put into action today. If you don't have time to execute your plan today, be sure to make it happen first thing tomorrow morning.

   a. _____

   _____

   b. _____

   _____

2. When it comes to outlook, do you fall on the positive or the negative side of the fence? Having a positive attitude about life improves enthusiasm. To increase your enthusiasm, mindfully consider your day and write down two examples of your positive attitude and/or actions.

   a. _____

   _____

   b. _____

   _____

Please take time to review your previous HERO exercises. Research shows that reflecting on past thoughts about wellness further strengthens and solidifies your HERO wellness traits. The HERO exercises are intentionally repeated every 8 days because repetition is crucial to learning and incorporating new ideas.

Act enthusiastic and you will be enthusiastic.
~ *Dale Carnegie*

Daily Journaling Form

EXERCISE	Exercise 30 minutes <u>at least 3 days</u> per week for 30 days, aim for at least moderate intensity		
Type of Exercise		Duration	_____ minutes
Intensity	☐ Low	☐ Moderate	☐ High

MINDFULNESS	Practice mindfulness at least 10 minutes <u>at least 3 days</u> per week for 30 days
Today's Guided Meditation(s)	

SLEEP	Implement 4 or more of the 6 sleep hygiene practices <u>at least 3 days</u> per week for 30 days		
Implemented These Sleep Hygiene Practices	☐ No electronics 90 min before bed	☐ Sleep mask or blackout shades	☐ Regular bedtime
	☐ No napping	☐ Warm bath/shower prior to bed	☐ Avoid caffeine 10 hrs before bed

SOCIAL CONNECTEDNESS	Meet or call at least two friends or family members <u>at least 3 days</u> per week for 30 days	
Today's Social Contacts	**Friends** ☐ Call ☐ In-person	**Family** ☐ Call ☐ In-person

NUTRITION	Log your daily meals/snacks/beverages/ alcohol <u>at least 3 days</u> per week for 30 days	
Logged Meals/Snacks/Beverages/Alcohol	☐ Yes	☐ No
Strongly Recommended		
Implemented MIND Diet Principles	☐ Yes	☐ No
Practiced Mindful Meal Meditation	☐ Breakfast ☐ Lunch ☐ Dinner	

TODAY'S PROGRESS	
My Barrier(s)	
My Solution(s)	

HERO Exercises
Happiness • Enthusiasm • Resilience • Optimism

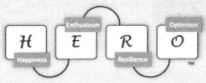

RESILIENCE & OPTIMISM FERTILIZE A POSITIVE ATTITUDE

1. Being of service to others is a great way to build resilience. List two things you did today (or will do tomorrow) to give back to others or to brighten their day.

    a. _____

    _____

    b. _____

    _____

2. Is your glass half-full or half-empty? How you view the world matters! Write down two things that happened today that you viewed as negative. Take a moment and give this some thought, and then write down a less negative, or even a positive interpretation of the same events.

    a. _____

    _____

    b. _____

    _____

Please take time to review your previous HERO exercises. Research shows that reflecting on past thoughts about wellness further strengthens and solidifies your HERO wellness traits. The HERO exercises are intentionally repeated every 8 days because repetition is crucial to learning and incorporating new ideas.

Optimism. It's not just a mind-set, it is behavior.
~ *Larry Elder*

Daily Journaling Form

EXERCISE	Exercise 30 minutes <u>at least 3 days</u> per week for 30 days, aim for at least moderate intensity	
Type of Exercise		Duration	_____ minutes
Intensity	☐ Low ☐ Moderate ☐ High	

MINDFULNESS	Practice mindfulness at least 10 minutes <u>at least 3 days</u> per week for 30 days
Today's Guided Meditation(s)	

SLEEP	Implement 4 or more of the 6 sleep hygiene practices <u>at least 3 days</u> per week for 30 days	
Implemented These Sleep Hygiene Practices	☐ No electronics 90 min before bed ☐ Sleep mask or blackout shades ☐ Regular bedtime	
	☐ No napping ☐ Warm bath/shower prior to bed ☐ Avoid caffeine 10 hrs before bed	

SOCIAL CONNECTEDNESS	Meet or call at least two friends or family members <u>at least 3 days</u> per week for 30 days	
	Friends	**Family**
Today's Social Contacts	☐ Call ☐ In-person	☐ Call ☐ In-person

NUTRITION	Log your daily meals/snacks/beverages/ alcohol <u>at least 3 days</u> per week for 30 days	
Logged Meals/Snacks/Beverages/Alcohol	☐ Yes ☐ No	
Strongly Recommended		
Implemented MIND Diet Principles	☐ Yes ☐ No	
Practiced Mindful Meal Meditation	☐ Breakfast ☐ Lunch ☐ Dinner	

TODAY'S PROGRESS	
My Barrier(s)	
My Solution(s)	

HERO Exercises
*H*appiness • *E*nthusiasm • *R*esilience • *O*ptimism

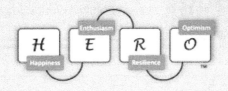

HAPPINESS & ENTHUSIASM PREDICT LOWER HEART RATE & BLOOD PRESSURE

---

1. Thinking about happy memories can positively impact your level of happiness! Write down two memories that bring a smile to your face. Next, spend a few minutes reliving each of these happy memories, and watch your current level of happiness increase.

    a. _____

    _____

    b. _____

    _____

2. Gratitude is known to increase feelings of happiness and enthusiasm. To increase these feelings, mindfully consider your day and write down two examples of things that happened today that increased your feelings of gratitude.

    a. _____

    _____

    b. _____

    _____

Please take time to review your previous HERO exercises. Research shows that reflecting on past thoughts about wellness further strengthens and solidifies your HERO wellness traits. The HERO exercises are intentionally repeated every 8 days because repetition is crucial to learning and incorporating new ideas.

Happiness, like unhappiness, is a proactive choice.
~ *Stephen Covey*

Daily Journaling Form

EXERCISE	Exercise 30 minutes <u>at least 3 days</u> per week for 30 days, aim for at least moderate intensity

Type of Exercise		Duration	_____ minutes
Intensity	☐ Low	☐ Moderate	☐ High

MINDFULNESS	Practice mindfulness at least 10 minutes <u>at least 3 days</u> per week for 30 days
Today's Guided Meditation(s)	

SLEEP	Implement 4 or more of the 6 sleep hygiene practices <u>at least 3 days</u> per week for 30 days

Implemented These Sleep Hygiene Practices	☐ No electronics 90 min before bed	☐ Sleep mask or blackout shades	☐ Regular bedtime
	☐ No napping	☐ Warm bath/shower prior to bed	☐ Avoid caffeine 10 hrs before bed

SOCIAL CONNECTEDNESS	Meet or call at least two friends or family members <u>at least 3 days</u> per week for 30 days

Today's Social Contacts	Friends		Family	
	☐ Call	☐ In-person	☐ Call	☐ In-person

NUTRITION	Log your daily meals/snacks/beverages/ alcohol <u>at least 3 days</u> per week for 30 days

Logged Meals/Snacks/Beverages/Alcohol	☐ Yes	☐ No
Strongly Recommended		
Implemented MIND Diet Principles	☐ Yes	☐ No
Practiced Mindful Meal Meditation	☐ Breakfast ☐ Lunch ☐ Dinner	

TODAY'S PROGRESS	
My Barrier(s)	
My Solution(s)	

HERO Exercises
Happiness • Enthusiasm • Resilience • Optimism

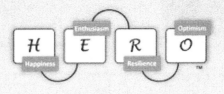

RESILIENCE & OPTIMISM ARE LINKED TO GREATER LIFE SATISFACTION

1. People are quick to point out faults and weaknesses. Acknowledging others' successes is a great way to build and strengthen your resilience while making another person feel great. Think of two people that have recently achieved some type of success, personal or work-related, and write down how you plan to acknowledge their achievement.

   a. _____

   _____

   b. _____

   _____

2. Have you heard of *Paying it Forward*? Someone does something kind for you and you pass it forward by doing something kind for another. Write down two times others have done something kind for you and how that made you feel. Make a plan to pass along those acts of kindness and brighten someone else's day.

   a. _____

   _____

   b. _____

   _____

Please take time to review your previous HERO exercises. Research shows that reflecting on past thoughts about wellness further strengthens and solidifies your HERO wellness traits. The HERO exercises are intentionally repeated every 8 days because repetition is crucial to learning and incorporating new ideas.

For every dark night, there's a brighter day.
~ Tupac

Daily Journaling Form

EXERCISE	Exercise 30 minutes at least 3 days per week for 30 days, aim for at least moderate intensity	
Type of Exercise	Duration	_____ minutes
Intensity	☐ Low ☐ Moderate ☐ High	

MINDFULNESS	Practice mindfulness at least 10 minutes at least 3 days per week for 30 days
Today's Guided Meditation(s)	

SLEEP	Implement 4 or more of the 6 sleep hygiene practices at least 3 days per week for 30 days		
Implemented These Sleep Hygiene Practices	☐ No electronics 90 min before bed	☐ Sleep mask or blackout shades	☐ Regular bedtime
	☐ No napping	☐ Warm bath/shower prior to bed	☐ Avoid caffeine 10 hrs before bed

SOCIAL CONNECTEDNESS	Meet or call at least two friends or family members at least 3 days per week for 30 days			
	Friends		Family	
Today's Social Contacts	☐ Call	☐ In-person	☐ Call	☐ In-person

NUTRITION	Log your daily meals/snacks/beverages/ alcohol at least 3 days per week for 30 days	
Logged Meals/Snacks/Beverages/Alcohol	☐ Yes	☐ No
Strongly Recommended		
Implemented MIND Diet Principles	☐ Yes	☐ No
Practiced Mindful Meal Meditation	☐ Breakfast ☐ Lunch ☐ Dinner	

TODAY'S PROGRESS	
My Barrier(s)	
My Solution(s)	

HERO Exercises
Happiness • Enthusiasm • Resilience • Optimism

HAPPINESS & ENTHUSIASM ARE LINKED TO LONGEVITY

1. To increase your happiness, let's work on strengthening your happiness muscle. Take a moment and write down two positive things that you'd like to experience today. Also, two to three times today, find a few minutes to visualize and relish these positive experiences.

   a. _____

   _____

   b. _____

   _____

2. Having a goal or a project that inspires you will increase your enthusiasm. Write down two projects you find inspiring and set a start date. Put the date on your calendar with reminder alerts – make it happen and watch your enthusiasm improve!

   a. _____

   _____

   b. _____

   _____

Please take time to review your previous HERO exercises. Research shows that reflecting on past thoughts about wellness further strengthens and solidifies your HERO wellness traits. The HERO exercises are intentionally repeated every 8 days because repetition is crucial to learning and incorporating new ideas.

There is no path to happiness: happiness is the path.
~ Buddha

Daily Journaling Form

EXERCISE	Exercise 30 minutes <u>at least 3 days</u> per week for 30 days, aim for at least moderate intensity

Type of Exercise		Duration	_____ minutes
Intensity	☐ Low	☐ Moderate	☐ High

MINDFULNESS	Practice mindfulness at least 10 minutes <u>at least 3 days</u> per week for 30 days
Today's Guided Meditation(s)	

SLEEP	Implement 4 or more of the 6 sleep hygiene practices <u>at least 3 days</u> per week for 30 days

Implemented These Sleep Hygiene Practices	☐ No electronics 90 min before bed	☐ Sleep mask or blackout shades	☐ Regular bedtime
	☐ No napping	☐ Warm bath/shower prior to bed	☐ Avoid caffeine 10 hrs before bed

SOCIAL CONNECTEDNESS	Meet or call at least two friends or family members <u>at least 3 days</u> per week for 30 days

Today's Social Contacts	Friends		Family	
	☐ Call	☐ In-person	☐ Call	☐ In-person

NUTRITION	Log your daily meals/snacks/beverages/ alcohol <u>at least 3 days</u> per week for 30 days

Logged Meals/Snacks/Beverages/Alcohol	☐ Yes	☐ No
Strongly Recommended		
Implemented MIND Diet Principles	☐ Yes	☐ No
Practiced Mindful Meal Meditation	☐ Breakfast ☐ Lunch ☐ Dinner	

TODAY'S PROGRESS	
My Barrier(s)	
My Solution(s)	

HERO Exercises
Happiness • Enthusiasm • Resilience • Optimism

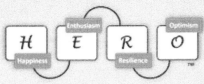

RESILIENT OPTIMISTS HAVE BETTER PHYSICAL HEALTH & BETTER RELATIONSHIPS

1. Resilience means the ability to bounce back from adversities. Write down 2 things about yourself that make you tough, and two skills you have used previously to overcome adversities. Remind yourself throughout the day that you genuinely possess these resilient traits.

   a. _____

   _____

   b. _____

   _____

2. Optimism often requires making a choice about how you view the world. Write down two positive things you want to happen tomorrow, and then spend a few minutes planning on how to make these optimistic attitudes/events a reality.

   a. _____

   _____

   b. _____

   _____

Please take time to review your previous HERO exercises. Research shows that reflecting on past thoughts about wellness further strengthens and solidifies your HERO wellness traits. The HERO exercises are intentionally repeated every 8 days because repetition is crucial to learning and incorporating new ideas.

What seems to us as bitter trials are often blessings in disguise.
~ Oscar Wilde

HERO Wellness Scale

Day 90

Now that you've finished the program, please complete the *HERO Wellness Scale*, found on the following page. Comparing your Day 1 and Day 90 HERO scores will allow you to measure the progress you made during your LiveWell90 journey.

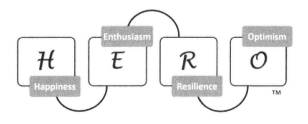

Phase 3: SUSTAIN **COMPLETE ON DAY 90** DATE: _____

HERO WELLNESS SCALE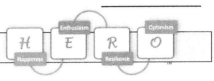

Please circle ONE NUMBER for each question below.

1. On average, during the last 7 DAYS, how happy have you felt?

0	1	2	3	4	5	6	7	8	9	10

Not at all happy   Mildly happy   Moderately happy   Highly happy   Extremely happy

2. On average, during the last 7 DAYS, how enthusiastic have you felt?

0	1	2	3	4	5	6	7	8	9	10

Not at all enthusiastic   Mildly enthusiastic   Moderately enthusiastic   Highly enthusiastic   Extremely enthusiastic

3. On average, during the last 7 DAYS, how resilient have you felt?

0	1	2	3	4	5	6	7	8	9	10

Not at all resilient   Mildly resilient   Moderately resilient   Highly resilient   Extremely resilient

4. On average, during the last 7 DAYS, how optimistic have you felt?

0	1	2	3	4	5	6	7	8	9	10

Not at all optimistic   Mildly optimistic   Moderately optimistic   Highly optimistic   Extremely optimistic

5. On average, during the last 7 DAYS, how would you rate your mental wellness?

0	1	2	3	4	5	6	7	8	9	10

Not at all good   Mildly good   Moderately good   Markedly good   Extremely good

- -

SCORING: To calculate total score, add all circled numbers.

TOTAL SCORE: 0 - 50

HIGHER SCORES INDICATE HIGHER LEVELS OF WELLNESS

SCORE

WILD 5★ **Wellness®**
Wellness Interventions for Life's Demands

© Copyright 2019 Saundra Jain & Rakesh Jain. All Rights Reserved.

REFLECTIONS and NEXT STEPS

We encourage you to document your *HERO Wellness Scale* scores below. Your scores will offer some insight into how your wellness changed throughout LiveWell90.

HERO Wellness Scale

Day 1: _____

Day 30: _____

Day 60: _____

Day 90: _____

Finally, we encourage you to take a moment to write about your LiveWell90 experiences. You might want to consider the following questions: *What did you learn about yourself during this 90-day wellness experience? How has your wellness improved? Was LiveWell90 worth the time and effort? Will you continue these wellness practices?*

_____

_____

_____

_____

_____

_____

_____

_____

To continue your wellness journey, please visit www.WILD5Wellness.com/forms to access copies of the program forms, which will help you with tracking, journaling, and assessing your wellness.

WILD 5 WELLNESS WARRIORS

Congratulations! You've successfully completed LiveWell90 and can proudly consider yourself a WILD 5 Wellness Warrior. You deserve a big pat on the back! Please take a moment and consider your accomplishments over the last 90 days. You've made some major emotional and behavioral changes and established many healthy habits. This wasn't an easy journey; it required dedication, commitment, persistence, patience, and a willingness to put yourself first. Don't let this monumental accomplishment slip by without acknowledging what you've achieved. We're very proud of you for taking such a big step towards achieving optimal mental and physical wellness.

Even though the formal program is complete, we encourage you to continue your wellness practices, strengthening them day-by-day. Remember, there is power in an integrated program, so we encourage you to continue all five of the wellness practices (exercise, mindfulness meditation, sleep, social connectedness, and nutrition), along with Daily Journaling, and the HERO exercises.

Keep your wellness workbook close at hand, relying on it as an ever-ready resource. If you slip in your wellness practices, remember to be kind to yourself. Simply shake it off, regroup, and begin again. We'd encourage you to review your *HERO Wellness Scale* scores as a reminder of your progress during the program.

If you'd like to be a part of a community of like-minded WILD 5 Wellness Warriors, we invite you to join our Facebook group. Email us at DrJain@WILD5Wellness.com and in the subject line, please write: I'd like to join the Facebook group. In the body of the email, please include your preferred email, and we will send you an invitation.

Our best to you in your continued pursuit of wellness!

Live Well,

Saundra
Saundra Jain, MA, PsyD, LPC

Rakesh
Rakesh Jain, MD, MPH

Saundra Jain, MA, PsyD, LPC, is a seasoned psychotherapist, educator, WebMD Blogger, and strong supporter of living a life based on wellness practices. Years of clinical practice and dealing with life's ups and downs have convinced her that wellness practices of exercise, mindfulness meditation, optimized sleep, social connectedness, and a nutritious diet are all essential wellness elements. She is the co-creator of WILD 5 Wellness.

Rakesh Jain, MD, MPH, is an experienced psychiatrist, researcher, and educator who firmly believes that life is much more than not having symptoms of mental illness. He believes that the attainment of mental wellness is our ultimate goal. Years of experience have taught him that mental wellness is a highly learnable skill and can be strengthened with practice. According to Dr. Jain, the purpose of WILD 5 Wellness is to help people deal with life's daily stresses and to flourish. He is the co-creator of WILD 5 Wellness.

Betsy Burns, PhD, is a clinical psychologist who has a personal and professional interest in wellness. For most of her career, she has worked with acutely ill, hospitalized psychiatric patients. In the last several years, her focus has broadened to include working with people who are interested in learning how to increase their overall sense of wellbeing.

Made in the USA
Coppell, TX
07 November 2020

40936934R00157